明代王朝 MING
THE GOLDEN EMPIRE

CATALOGUE NO. 55

Portrait of He Bin (dates unknown)

See pages 58–59

明代王朝 MING
THE GOLDEN EMPIRE

National Museums Scotland

MING
THE GOLDEN EMPIRE

Exhibition at:

National Museums Scotland

Chambers Street
Edinburgh EH1 1JF

www.nms.ac.uk

27 June to 19 October 2014

Produced by Nomad Exhibitions
in association with Nanjing
Museum

First published by
NMS Enterprises Limited – Publishing
a division of NMS Enterprises Limited
National Museums Scotland
Chambers Street
Edinburgh EH1 1JF

Catalogue format and additional material
© National Museums Scotland 2014

Source of images (as credited)

British Library Cataloguing in Publication Data

A catalogue record for this book is available from the
British Library.

ISBN 978-1-905267-90-3

Project management and design by NMS Enterprises
       Limited – Publishing.
Cover layout by Mark Blackadder.
Cover images: See catalogue nos 34 and 136.
Printed and bound in the United Kingdom by Bell & Bain
       Limited, Glasgow.

CONTENTS

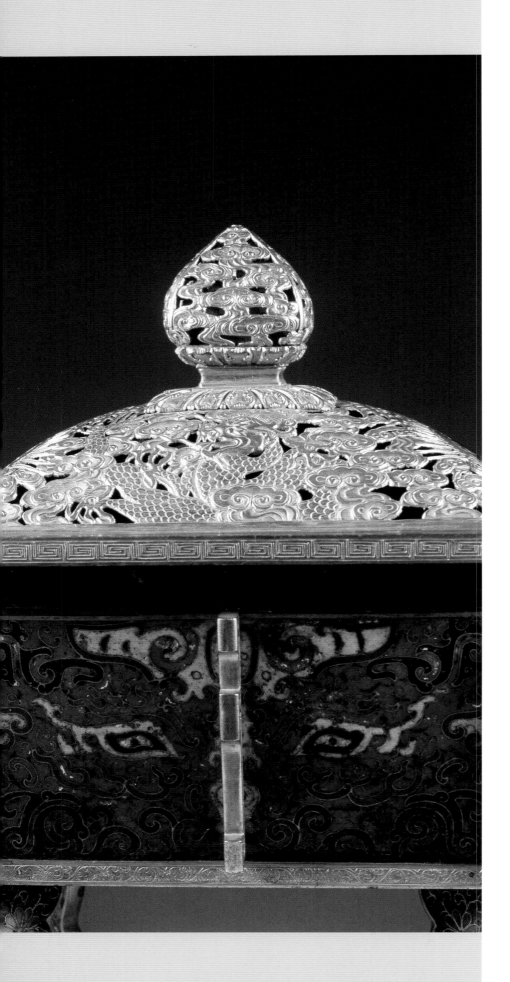

CATALOGUE NO. 19

Cloisonné incense-burner (*fang-ding*).

See page 19

FOREWORD

明
代
王
朝

We are delighted to host in Scotland this special exhibition of original Ming artefacts from Nanjing Museum. This is the only venue for the exhibition in the United Kingdom and it will be on show from 27 June until 19 October 2014.

The exhibition offers a rich cornucopia of material from the three centuries of the extraordinarily successful Ming dynasty which ruled China from 1368 until 1644. Under a succession of powerful rulers this empire flourished and with it a spectacular culture demonstrative of great sophistication and wealth.

The imperial court led the way with its appetite for works of art, fine porcelain, silk, and ornaments of jade and cloisonné enamels, as well as its reverence for scholarship. The beautiful blue and white porcelain, now synonymous with the Ming era, was produced in quantity and was far superior in quality to its contemporary European equivalent. For the first fifty years of the period, Nanjing was the capital. Later, successive emperors created and elaborated the palace which was to become the Forbidden City in Beijing.

This exhibition includes some wonderful items of porcelain, jade and bronze from the collections of National Museums Scotland. Their presence in Scottish national collections shows the enduring fascination in the West with the culture of China.

We thank Nanjing Museum and Nomad Exhibitions for making this exhibition possible in co-operation with our staff.

Dr Gordon Rintoul OBE
National Museums Scotland
June 2014

CATALOGUE NO. 34

A piece of silk brocade used for making
dragon robes.

See pages 30–31

MING
THE GOLDEN EMPIRE

CATALOGUE

This publication has been
produced with kind support from

Mr Campbell Armour and Mr Angus McLeod

EXHIBITION

National Museums Scotland
would like to thank

Baillie Gifford Investment Managers

for their generous sponsorship of the exhibition.

BAILLIE GIFFORD

INVESTMENT MANAGERS

DYNASTIC CHRONOLOGY

Shang		*ca.*1600–1046 BC	商
Zhou		*ca.*1046–256 BC	周
	Western Zhou	*ca.*1046–771 BC	西周
	Eastern Zhou	770–256 BC	東周
	Spring and Autumn period	770–476 BC	春秋
	Warring States period	475–221 BC	戰國
Qin		221–206 BC	秦
Han		206 BC–AD 220	漢朝
	Western Han	202 BC–AD 23	西漢 (前漢)
	Eastern Han	25–220	東漢 (後漢)
Six Dynasties		220–589	六朝
	Three Kingdoms period	220–280	三國
	Western Jin	265–316	西晉
	Eastern Jin	317–420	東晉
	Northern and Southern dynasties	420–589	南北朝
Sui		581–618	隋
Tang		618–907	唐
Five Dynasties		902–979	五代十國
Liao (Qidan)		916–1125	遼
Jin (Jurchen)		1115–1234	金
Song		960–1279	宋
	Northern Song	960–1127	北宋
	Southern Song	1127–1279	南宋
Yuan (Mongol)		1279–1368	元 (蒙古)
Ming		1368–1644	明
Qing (Manchu)		1644–1911	清 (滿州)

EMPERORS OF THE MING DYNASTY

1. Zhu Yuanzhang 朱元璋
(personal name)

Taizu 太祖 (temple name)
Hongwu 洪武 (Abundantly Martial)
(reign title)
1328–1398 (life years)
1368–1398 (reign years)
Hongwu emperor (commonly used title)

2. Zhu Yunwen 朱允炆

Huizong 惠宗
Jianwen 建文 (Establishing Civility)
1377–1402
1399–1402
Jianwen emperor

3. Zhu Di 朱棣

Chengzu 成祖
Yongle 永樂 (Eternal Happiness)
1360–1424
1402–1424
Yongle emperor

4. Zhu Gaochi 朱高熾

Renzong 仁宗
Hongxi 洪熙 (Vast Splendour)
1378–1425
1425
Hongxi emperor

5. Zhu Zhanji 朱瞻基

Xuanzong 宣宗
Xuande 宣德 (Propagating Virtue)
1398–1435
1426–1435
 Xuande emperor

6. Zhu Qizhen 朱祁鎮

Yingzong 英宗
Zhengtong 正統 (Rectified Unity)
1427–1464
1436–1449
Zhengtong emperor

7. Zhu Qiyu 朱祁鈺

Daizong 代宗
Jingtai 景泰 (Bright Exaltation)
1428–1457
1450–1456
Jingtai emperor

8. Zhu Qizhen 朱祁鎮

Yingzong 英宗
Tianshun 天順 (Obedient to Heaven)
1427–1464
1456–1464
Zhengtong emperor

9. Zhu Jianshen 朱見深

Xianzong 憲宗
Chenghua 成化 (Accomplish
Transformation)
1447–1487
1465–1487
Chenghua emperor

10. Zhu Youcheng 朱祐樘

Xiaozong 孝宗
Hongzhi 弘治 (Firm Rule)
1470–1505
1488–1505
Hongzhi emperor

11. Zhu Houzhao 朱厚照

Wuzong 武宗
Zhengde 正德 (Rectifying Virtue)
1491–1521
1506–1521
Zhengde emperor

12. Zhu Houcong 朱厚熜

Shizong 世宗
Jiajing 嘉靖 (Excellent Tranquillity)
1507–1567
1522–1566
Jiajing emperor

13. Zhu Zaihou 朱載坖

Muzong 穆宗
Longqing 隆慶 (Effulgent Felicitations)
1537–1572
1567–1572
Longqing emperor

14. Zhu Yijun 朱翊鈞

Shenzong 神宗
Wanli 萬曆 (Eternal Chronometry)
1563–1520
1573–1620
Wanli emperor

15. Zhu Changluo 朱常洛

Guangzong 光宗
Taichang 泰昌 (Great Prosperity)
1582–1620
1620
Taichang emperor

16. Zhu Youjiao 朱由校

Xizong 熹宗
Tianqi 天啟 (Opening to Heaven)
1605–1627
1621–1627
Tianqi emperor

17. Zhu Youjian 朱由檢

Sizong 思宗
Chongzhen 崇禎 (Exalted Auspiciousness)
1611–1644
1628–1644
Chongzhen emperor

CATALOGUE NO. 140

Hexagonal vase with floral decoration.

See page 132

AN INTRODUCTION
TO THE NANJING MUSEUM

明
代
王
朝

Founding and history

The Nanjing Museum was founded in 1933 at the instigation of
Cai Yuanpei (1868–1940), then Minister for Education, President
of Academia Sinica (founded in 1928), and a leading light in Chinese
liberal education during the early 20th century. In 1935, a site was
purchased for the Nanjing Museum in the park surrounding the
Chaotian Palace (*Chaotian Gong*), known as Zhongshan Half
Mountain Park. The Chaotian Palace had originally been an imperial
palace built by the Hongwu emperor (r. 1368–1398) in the late
14th century, and the Museum still remains on the same site today.
Storage facilities were built here and completed in 1936. Construction
of storage for the new Museum began in March 1936 and was completed in December of that year.

On 1 January 1937, the Nanjing Museum was opened as a branch
of the Palace Museum in Beijing when it was known as the National
Central Museum Preparatory Office. In 1949 this title was changed
to the National Central Museum, and in March 1950 it was again
renamed the National Nanjing Museum, with the title of Nanjing
Museum finally being settled upon in 1959.

It was initially proposed that the Museum have three exhibition
galleries dedicated to Natural History, Humanities, and Technology,
but political instability and the outbreak of war meant that only the
gallery dedicated to the Humanities was ever built. Construction of
the Museum was interrupted in 1937 with the start of the Second
Sino-Japanese War (1937–1945), and it was only finally completed
at the end of 1947.

The origins of the Nanjing Museum can be traced to events that
took place in Beijing's Forbidden City in the late 1920s. After the
collapse of the Qing dynasty in 1911, the last Qing emperor Puyi
(1906–1967) continued to live in the Forbidden City, the last of the
24 Ming and Qing emperors who had occupied the Forbidden City
since 1420. Here he stayed, along with a few remaining members of
the imperial family and an entourage of kinsmen and servants, until
their expulsion by the Nationalist General Feng Yuxiang (1882–1948)
in November 1924.

During the years since the fall of the Qing, the imperial collections
housed in the Forbidden City – the result of imperial collecting since
the Song dynasty (960–1279), suffered from serious theft by eunuchs
and officials, and dispersal as gifts or sale by Puyi. Countless works of
art from the imperial collection were lost in this way. During 1924 and
1925 the Nationalist government arranged for the surviving imperial

collection to be inventoried, and in 1925 the Palace Museum was established in the Forbidden City, opening to the public on 10 October of that year.

In 1931, the Japanese invaded and overran China's northeast, known at that time as Manchuria. The Museum's then Director Yi Peiji (1880–1937) took the decision to relocate the collections south, in the event that the Japanese invaded south of the Great Wall. Some 20,000 carefully packed crates thus left the Forbidden City in 1933, first to Shanghai and then in 1936 to Nanjing, at that time the capital of the Nationalist government. In 1937, as the Japanese advanced into southern China, further dispersals of the imperial collection took place to the caves and temples of Sichuan and Guizhou.

Following the Japanese defeat in 1945, these were then returned to Nanjing in 1947, coinciding with the resumption of the Civil War (1946–1950) between Chinese Communist and Nationalist forces.

Collections

In late 1948 and early 1949, some of the imperial collections stored at Nanjing were shipped to Taipei in Taiwan with the fleeing Nationalists to become part of the holdings of the National Palace Museum, Taipei. Following the founding in 1949 of the People's Republic of China, most of the Palace Museum material that had been stored in the Nanjing Museum was returned in the early 1950s, although 2211 crates of material remained, mostly of ceramics and decorative arts.

Today, a much smaller, although still very significant, amount of imperial material remains in the Nanjing Museum's collections. In 1936, the Museum incorporated first the Historical Museum of the Academia Sinica, and in 1959 the collections of the Jiangsu Provincial Museum.

The Nanjing Museum is now one of the largest museums in China, with over 420,000 artefacts in its holdings. Its collections of Ming and Qing porcelain are particularly outstanding. These number some 200,000 artefacts, making them among the most extensive of such collections in the world. It also has vast collections of ceramics from earlier periods, which reflect a continuing programme of active archaeological excavations. The Museum's calligraphy and painting collections, which consist of c.38,000 works, are also especially significant and feature many masterpieces by historic and modern artists. In addition, the Nanjing Museum's diverse holdings boast

outstanding collections of early bronzes, Buddhist material, lacquer, jades, textiles, inscription rubbings, gold and silver metalwork, statuary, and carving in a range of materials.

The Nanjing Museum today

The Nanjing Museum functions today as a national as well as a provincial level museum, and increasingly plays an international role in the promotion of Chinese history and culture. The importance and prestige of this role is reflected in the Museum's most recent phase of development which commenced in 2009, and has seen its buildings expand to 85,000 square meters at a cost of 700 million *renminbi*, with an additional 300 million being spent on outfitting exhibition halls.

This phase of development, due to open to the public in 2014, has involved either new construction or extension of the existing Museum buildings, with six exhibition halls to include the History Museum, Art Gallery, Exhibition Hall, Hall of the Republic of China, Cultural Heritage Hall, and Digital Library. In addition, six research institutes are attached to the Nanjing Museum: for Jiangsu Provincial Archaeology, Cultural Relic Protection, Ancient Architecture, Ancient Cultural Heritage, Ancient Art, and Visual Art Exhibition.

In Chinese, the Nanjing Museum is known as the *Nanjing Bowuyuan*, with *bowuyuan* – as opposed to *bowuguan*, the usual word in Chinese for 'museum' – a term of special significance reserved for only three institutions in the Chinese-speaking world: the Palace Museum in Beijing, the National Palace Museum in Taipei, and the Nanjing Museum. These three institutions, each with unparalleled collections, were the main inheritors of the Qing imperial collections, and as such occupy unique and prestigious institutional roles in the interpretation of China's imperial heritage through their collections in the 21st century.

FURTHER READING

Elliot and Shambaugh 2005;
Gong 2014; Li 2013

CATALOGUE NO. 15

The Forbidden City and its architect, Kuai Xiang (1398–1481).

See page 16

THE ORIGINS OF THE MING

明
代
王
朝

The Ming dynasty lasted for nearly three centuries, during which time 16 emperors of the Zhu family reigned over the world's largest, wealthiest and most populous empire. This was a period during which art, literature, culture, scholarship and technological development flourished, each distinguished by new heights of innovation, creativity and achievement. The Ming economy transformed itself from a primarily agrarian economy in the late 14th and early 15th centuries into one that had a significantly greater commercial and market focus by the 16th century, with an attendant boom in economic prosperity. These factors, combined with the unity, stability and lack of any serious external threats experienced by the Ming, meant that the population grew from an estimated 60 million at the dynasty's outset to approximately 175 million by the time of its fall – a change which was not without considerable impact on the ecology of the natural environment as more cultivatable land, and more resources, were needed to support the expanding population. This essay will provide a very brief introduction to the Ming dynasty, outlining its origins, and in broad outline the nature and patterns of Ming imperial rule.

The origins of the Ming lie in the preceding Mongol-ruled Yuan dynasty (1279–1368), a dynasty that had been distinguished by harsh and discriminatory rule. The hierarchical Yuan state conceived of four levels of citizen – with Mongols at the top of Yuan society; followed by Central Asian peoples from the Mongol empire (1206–1368); then northern Chinese which included Han, Khitan and Jurchen peoples linked with the Mongol world; and finally southern Chinese, who had remained under the rule of the Southern Song (1127–1279).

In 1344 an outbreak of bubonic plague, known as the Black Death, originated in Central Asia and swept across Eurasia, devastating populations in its wake. In China there was a succession of enormous famines that combined with droughts and floods, resulting in a decimated and struggling Chinese population (estimated to be around 130 million during the early 13th century before the hardships brought about by Mongol rule, plague, famine and drought). Sectarian and millenarian movements grew in response to these disasters, the largest of which were the Red Turbans, a popular name for a millenarian Buddhist group whose soldiers were identified by red headbands. The Red Turbans believed that at the moment of humanity's greatest darkness and despair, the future Buddha, Maitreya Buddha, would appear, to bring about a reversal of humankind's fortunes.

Lawlessness, banditry and unrest became a widespread feature of late Yuan life. By the 1350s there were numerous large-scale anti-Yuan

uprisings occurring mainly in central China, with some rebel and bandit groups coalescing into larger armies rebelling against Mongol rule. One such Red Turban army, based in the Yangzi river valley and led by the warlord Zhu Yuanzhang (1328–1398), succeeded in capturing Nanjing in 1356. Here Zhu set up an administration to govern the areas under his control, recruiting eminent scholars who had served under the Yuan to advise his growing administration. He then went on to defeat several rival warlords during a period in which China endured what was effectively a widespread civil war. Zhu succeeded in expelling the Mongols from their capital Khanbaliq (Dadu, or present-day Beijing), and forced them to retreat entirely from northern China back to their hereditary steppes.

In 1368, Zhu founded a new dynasty – the Ming. This was the first time in the 241 years since the collapse of the Northern Song (960–1127) that a native Chinese dynasty had succeeded in ruling all of China. It was also to be the last native Han dynasty, since the Ming would be succeeded by the Manchu-ruled Qing dynasty (1644–1911). As dynasties ruled by non-Han peoples, both the Yuan and Qing are sometimes referred to as alien dynasties.

The Ming founder

The founder of the Ming, Zhu Yuanzhang, was born on 21 October 1328 to a peasant family in the village of Zhongli, Haozhou County (present-day Fengyang), in Anhui province. He proved to be one of the most remarkable emperors in Chinese history and one of a rare few to have risen from such a humble background. Zhu appears to have been highly intelligent, becoming initially a remarkable military leader and then, as emperor, a highly capable and industrious, if at times brutal, administrator. In 1344, at the age of 16, he saw almost all his family succumb to a smallpox epidemic which left him with disfigured features.

Zhu joined a Buddhist monastery, the Huangjue Temple, and for a number of years became a mendicant Buddhist novice monk, before returning in 1348 to the monastery where he gained at least a basic level of literacy. When, in 1352, the monastery was burned down by Mongol troops searching for Red Turban rebels, Zhu joined the Red Turbans. He proved to be an effective, courageous and astute military leader, methodically building his power base and rising to leadership through the ranks. Zhu's armies increased in size quickly; after 1363 he no longer led his armies on the field, but left them in the hands of his generals.

Throughout the 1360s, Zhu became increasingly disassociated from the Red Turbans until, in 1366, he broke with them completely.

When Zhu founded his new dynasty at Nanjing, he named it Ming, or in Chinese, *Da Ming*, meaning 'Great Brightness'. As a man of war, he chose as his reign name *Hongwu*, meaning 'Abundantly Martial', to reflect his military priorities in the face of a continuing Mongol threat.

Zhu Yuanzhang, now the Hongwu emperor, immediately set about the task of reforming and governing this new dynasty with great energy and efficiency. In cultural terms, the Ming meant a reassertion of native Han Chinese values – a return to the glories of pre-Mongol China – by attempting to rid China of 'barbarian' Mongol influences, such as Mongol dress. Hongwu instituted sumptuary regulations that forbade Mongol hair and clothing styles and reinstituted Tang (618–907) and Song (960–1279) styles of dress.

In practice though, the Mongol legacy continued into the Ming in a number of ways, notably in government organization and in the structure of provinces inherited from the Yuan.

The six main Ministries of Ming government were Revenue, Personnel, Rites, War, Punishments and Works. These were all overseen by a Secretariat consisting of grand councillors and a chancellor in a prime-ministerial role. In 1380 the Secretariat was abolished by Hongwu when he felt threatened by the power the then chancellor Hu Weiyong (d.1380) had abrogated to himself. Hongwu had Hu Weiyong executed for treason and initiated a series of bloody purges of anyone even remotely connected to him; some 40,000 people are estimated to have lost their lives as a result. Then, in 1385, due to a grain corruption scandal, 10,000 people died; later, in 1393, 15,000 died during another purge. These purges continued over 14 years, during which time the Hongwu emperor destroyed anyone who came under suspicion, taking a particularly heavy toll among the educated literati who administered the country.

The emperor's autocratic, excessively cruel and despotic attitude toward dissent had already become evident during the late 1360s when Hongwu had taken brutal action against China's economic and cultural heartland in the lower Yangzi delta region – known as Jiangnan – which had been ruled by a powerful rival warlord. This took the form of banishments, imprisonments, deportations of wealthy households, punitive taxation and the execution of many of the Jiangnan élite, the effects of which took the Jiangnan region generations to recover from. One of the legacies of Hongwu's purges was a highly autocratic and centralized state in which all aspects of Ming life were subordinate to the emperor.

The story of the early Ming is one dominated by the Hongwu emperor and his vision for Ming society, which was strongly shaped by the chaos and warfare Hongwu had experienced under the Mongols. He envisaged a peaceful, stable and self-sufficient agrarian society in which people had little need to venture beyond their home villages. This austere vision of society had little use for commerce, or for specialized production, and did not take account of, or allow for, the changes that Ming society inevitably underwent. Hongwu adopted his new role as Son of Heaven with the utmost zealousness, and few aspects of the administration of his new empire escaped his interest.

In 1381 Hongwu required that his officials register and record every individual and their land-holdings in what were known as the Yellow Registers. This census documented the name, age and birthplace of every household head, as well as their land and animal holdings, size of residence, and their occupational category. Once recorded, the occupational categories of families remained fixed and permanent. Associated with the Yellow Registers was the formation in 1381 of the *lijia* system (similar to the medieval English hundred and tithing), a system whereby households were grouped into units of 110 for the purposes of assessing and collecting tax, labour levy, and the distribution of government services.

In 1387 a second registration and tax assessment system was implemented to gather information on the size and productivity of landholdings. These were known as Fish-Scale Registers because the drawings of land plots contained therein resembled the overlapping scales of a fish.

Hongwu's vision of rural communities living in a self-sustaining pastoral idyll never became a reality as both the Ming economy and society changed and became far more market-orientated and ever more connected. Villages became tied into regional and national market networks, and the formation of religious, lineage, schools and other community organizations served to reduce the isolation of Ming village society as the dynasty progressed. Eventually the changes in society and economy were officially acknowledged in the late 16th-century tax reform known as the Single-Whip Tax, in which a variety of taxes in kind were consolidated into a single payment in silver, thus conceding the reality of the late Ming's monetized economy. Among the changes brought about by the introduction of the Single-Whip Tax were an increase in wage payments for labour, a decrease in levy labour, and greater simplicity in a tax system which had become over-burdened with inequities, abuses, rates of commutation, levies and the difficulty of collecting tax arrears.

The Ming palace complexes

Hongwu established his capital at Yingtian, a city on the Yangzi River, making it his dynastic capital in 1368. A new palace complex was constructed, and the city wall extended to become the longest in Ming China. It took *ca*.21 years to complete, and was *ca*.38 kilometres long, 12 metres high, and 7.5 metres wide. (By 1400 Nanjing's population is estimated to have been around one million, making it probably the largest city in the world at that time.)

The third Ming emperor, Yongle (r.1402–1424), increasingly conscious of the Mongol threat in the north, moved the capital to the former Yuan capital at Dadu in 1420, which was much better placed strategically for defensive or offensive military actions against the Mongols. Dadu was renamed Beijing (literally 'Northern Capital'), and Yingtian then renamed Nanjing (literally 'Southern Capital') to function as the Ming auxiliary capital.

Built between 1406 and 1420, the Beijing palace complex, or Forbidden City, enclosed the Inner Court, imperial residences and government offices. These two immense new imperial palace complexes at Nanjing and Beijing, constructed during the early Ming, required furnishing and decorating to the highest standards. A million conscript or convict labourers worked on its construction, with 100,000 craftsmen estimated to have worked on the timber, stone-carving and other decorative elements of the palace complex. The materials used in the building work came from all over the Ming empire, and it is estimated that 2 per cent of the 15th-century Ming population contributed to, or were in some way, involved in the creation of the Forbidden City.

A number of large and costly supporting and infrastructure projects were undertaken during the early Ming in order to support the relocation of the capital to Beijing. In 1415 the Grand Canal that linked Hangzhou with Beijing was repaired to improve the shipping of tax grain and goods to Beijing. The Grand Canal also became a major trade artery as Beijing was far from the cultural, economic and agricultural centres of southern and southeast China and required almost every necessity shipped to it. The link was also used by the government courier system. The mid-Ming official Li Dongyang (1447–1516) recorded that the number of official grain barges heading to the capital annually numbered over 10,000, with private boats and merchant barges being too numerous to count.

With the relocation of the capital to Beijing, construction also began on the imperial mausoleums, known as the Ming Imperial Tombs, which are located on the north-western edge of Beijing. Thirteen Ming emperors would be interred there. The Great Wall was also substantially reconstructed and garrisoned to defend the northern border against the Mongols, a threat that continued throughout the dynasty.

The main audience halls and gates of the Forbidden City were built on a north-south alignment, reflecting an architectural tradition described in texts dating from the Zhou dynasty. The imperial throne was located facing south on this axis, connecting the emperor as Son of Heaven in a geometry of celestial alignment with the empire over which he ruled. Belief in the Mandate of Heaven as personified in the emperor as Son of Heaven, had been a central idea in Chinese political thought for millennia. It was premised upon the idea of a just ruler, and the Mandate of Heaven was believed to have been withdrawn when a ruler failed in his duties and a dynasty collapsed. Natural, supernatural and man-made omens and portents were all read as indicators of Heaven's favour. These might include large-scale natural disasters such as floods or earthquakes, eclipses, unseasonal or freakish weather, outbreaks of peasant uprisings or epidemic illness. Officials were expected to record these events and to notify central government.

Rites were essential to affirm the emperor's role as Son of Heaven and preserve the moral authority to rule. These were extensive and various, and were

required to be performed correctly and at specified times throughout the year. The many rites of the Ming imperial court, which included investitures, funerals and seasonal sacrifices, were carefully compiled and described in great detail in court handbooks. The major rites of the Ming state religion, sacrifices to Heaven, Earth, and to the imperial ancestors, were held at dedicated altars and temples around Beijing.

From 1420, Beijing remained the Ming capital for 224 years and a succession of 14 Ming emperors lived within Beijing's Forbidden City, which had been patterned on the Nanjing palace complex. The Forbidden City was divided into two large compartmentalized sections with the northern Inner Court housing the imperial residences and used for day-to-day administration; the southern Outer Court was used for ceremonial business. The Inner and Outer Courts were enclosed within the massive outer ten-metre high vermillion painted wall of the Forbidden City, which was in turn surrounded by a broad moat about 52 metres wide. Immediately south of the Forbidden City lay the bureaus, agencies and ministries of Ming central government.

The composition of the imperial court reflected both the ethnic diversity of the Ming and the international nature of contacts beyond its borders. It consisted of not only the imperial family – the emperor, princes, princesses, empresses, dowager empresses, concubines and imperial relatives – but also foreign emissaries, officials, imperial tutors, artists, artisans and craftsmen, entertainers, Tibetan Buddhist monks, Mongol warriors, Korean palace women, eunuchs and many more.

As the only male attendants permitted to live in the Inner Court, eunuchs played a central role in managing and supervising the imperial household. Most were castrated before the age of ten, and they often came from very poor families. They were the only males, apart from the emperor, allowed access to the areas of the Inner Court populated by the imperial consorts and concubines. Widely despised,

especially by Confucian officials, they were responsible only to the emperor. Hongwu had greatly limited the role of eunuchs at court and had given instructions that they should hold no power and have no ability to interfere in the processes of administration. To this end he sought to keep their numbers low, and their literacy at a minimal level. However, they proved too useful as they had the ability to carry out roles not easily tasked to other areas of the administration. Their numbers grew, and they often occupied unique positions of power and were sometimes entrusted by emperors with influential state roles. At times during the Ming, their power and wealth became so great that they were seen as a threat to the existence of the Ming state by the Confucian-educated officials who administered it, and with whom eunuch factions increasingly came into conflict in the latter stages of the dynasty.

Among the most feared and notorious eunuchs was Wei Zhongxian (1568–1627), who virtually ruled China during the reign of the Tianqi emperor (1621–1627), and who was opposed most openly by conservative Confucian scholars of the Donglin Academy political faction, many of whom Wei Zhongxian had arrested, tortured and killed.

By the late Ming, 10–12,000 eunuchs worked in the Forbidden City, many in minor domestic roles, some in technical support roles, and others in administrative capacities. They became, as a result, expert in the bureaucratic and institutional procedures of the court. During the same period, some 50,000 or more eunuchs also served in a variety of roles outside Beijing, many in a military capacity.

The tribute system

Among the most famous eunuchs of the Ming was Zheng He (1371–1433), an admiral who undertook seven vast expeditionary sea-voyages between 1405 and 1433 to southeast and south Asia, and to east

Africa. These were part of an effort by the Yongle emperor to extend the tribute system, the formalized diplomatic practice in which the Ming saw itself as central and superior to other states and peoples, and sought to gain recognition and acknowledgement of the Ming by those states and peoples.

Tributary members sent embassies to the imperial court, acknowledging the superiority of Chinese culture, and in turn they received gifts, recognition, trade rights with China, and some military protection. The list of tribute states included countries that Hongwu forbade the Ming to invade, such as Japan, Korea, the Ryukus, Annam, Champa, Cambodia, Java and Brunei. Although the tribute system applied more to members neighbouring the Ming, and was the system under which official external trade was technically administered and managed by the Ministry of Rites, the tribute system was never intended as a trade system; the Ming state did not see much advantage in foreign trade. The gifts given in return to tribute embassies, for example, often far outweighed the value of gifts brought by the tribute embassies. And these embassies could be extremely large, with mid-15th century Jurchen (later to become the Manchu) missions, for example, numbering 3000 to 4000 men.

Art of the Ming imperial court

Ming imperial court art was an art of patronage: it reflected the emperor's taste and legitimized his role and position. Overseen by eunuchs, workshops in Beijing and elsewhere produced countless objects for imperial use. These included furniture, metalwork, jades, textiles, lacquer, cloisonné and porcelains.

The colour, form and decoration of these objects and materials needed to be of a quality appropriate for use in an imperial palace. Strict supervision ensured that objects created for the imperial court were produced to very precise and exacting specifications. Auspicious motifs, dragons, phoenixes, and

Buddhist and Daoist symbols, decorated the surfaces of most objects and materials used within imperial contexts. These motifs, symbols and colours combined to form a rich visual language that served to assert visible expressions of imperial virtue, rank, authority and legitimacy. Dragons and phoenixes, which represented male *yang* and female *yin* principles, featured prominently and prolifically in the visual language of the imperial court arts. Five-clawed dragons, in particular, were exclusively restricted to imperial use and forbidden to Ming commoners.

Porcelains, with ritual, banquet, functional and decorative use, were among the most influential objects to have been produced for the Ming court. The forms and glazes of imperial porcelains changed from reign to reign over the course of the dynasty, in response to the changing tastes and needs of the court. Imperial porcelains were exclusively produced at the imperial factory kilns at Jingdezhen, northern Jiangxi province, which supplied the palaces exclusively. No expense was spared in the production of ceramics of outstanding quality, and the Jingdezhen kilns had access to high quality clays restricted for imperial use.

During the early Ming, cobalt, used to paint the blue designs on blue and white porcelain, was imported from Persia. From the early 15th century, this was replaced with locally sourced cobalt. Vast orders were placed by the imperial court, with one request in 1433 itemizing 443,500 items. During the Jiajing reign (1522–1566), over one million pieces of porcelain were required, and annual orders exceeding 100,000 pieces seem to have been the norm.

Although the Ming court did not reintroduce a formal imperial painting academy modelled on those of the Northern and Southern Song dynasty, professional painters were still appointed to the Ming imperial court to fulfil its painting requirements. Indeed, the court became a very significant centre of painting production during the early to mid-Ming period.

Court-appointed painters were given nominal titles in the imperial bodyguard, known as the Embroidered Uniform Guard, where they might be awarded a variety of titles and ranks. Appointed to a number of halls and palaces throughout the Forbidden City, court painters produced art to embellish the new imperial palace, with suitable ideological or historical narrative themes reflecting the political legitimacy of the Ming. Their work might also serve a decorative function, with paintings of flowers-and-birds or seasonal landscapes, for example. The work was often large-scale and painted on silk, and might be elaborately detailed and highly coloured as it was required to occupy prominent positions within the many halls of the Forbidden City.

To supply the day-to-day needs of the imperial court, court-appointed painters might be required to work on imperial portraits, religious and ceremonial images, paintings intended for personal or diplomatic exchange expressing symbolic messages of good wishes or congratulation, or art that fulfilled a documentary role by recording ceremonial activities and official visits of the emperor.

The numbers of painters appointed to the court expanded greatly over the 15th century, becoming a cause of resentment and jealousy among officials. However, the ascension of the Jiajing emperor to the throne in 1522, as the result of what is known as the Great Rites Controversy (a dispute between the Jiajing emperor and his senior officials over the line of imperial succession) led to a decline in the fortunes of the Ming imperial painting academy, with almost no painters remaining at court by 1530.

The style in which court artists predominantly worked was the academic manner favoured by the Northern and Southern Song dynasty imperial courts, thus evoking the standards of a golden age of Chinese painting. By the time of the Ming imperial court academy's decline in the early 16th century, the wealthy and cultured élite of Suzhou, Hangzhou, Nanjing, Yangzhou and other wealthy southern cities of the Jiangnan region, increasingly defined art, taste and patronage.

Decline and fall: the late Ming

The early Ming had been a period of rebuilding and renewal in the aftermath of the famines, droughts, epidemics and anti-Mongol rebellions witnessed by China during the late 14th century. It was also a time of projecting the new power and prestige of the Ming through overseas expeditions and trade. A number of active and capable emperors during the early Ming led to a reinvigoration of Chinese polity, society and culture. The mid-Ming period, from the mid-15th to the mid-16th century, saw the Ming state becoming increasingly isolationist and inward-looking.

A significant catalyst in this had been the military debacle at a place called Tumu, a six-day march north-west of Beijing. Here, in 1449, at the behest of powerful court eunuchs, the 22-year-old Zhengtong emperor (r.1436–1449) led a force of 500,000 against a far smaller army of Oirat Mongols. The Ming force was almost totally annihilated by the Mongols, and the Zhengtong emperor was taken hostage in Mongolia. When news reached Beijing, some officials fled south in the resulting panic. The Mongols then attempted, unsuccessfully, to ransom the captured emperor and eventually released him after four years.

The emperor's capture presented the Ming state with a constitutional crisis, which was eventually resolved by appointing his younger brother as the Jingtai emperor (r.1450–1456). Jingtai was later deposed, rumoured to have been strangled by eunuchs, and the Zhengtong emperor reinstated under the reign title of Tianshun, following a *coup d'état* in 1457.

The late Ming period, from the mid-16th century onwards, was marked by weak emperors, passivity, poor administration, decadence and corruption. The reign of the Wanli emperor (r.1573–1620) is usually noted as a turning point in the history of the later period, when the Wanli emperor effectively lost interest in his administration and refused to deal with his officials, except through eunuch intermediaries. The Ming government consequently entered into decline, with many officials resigning or abandoning their posts.

Costly Ming military campaigns, fought against the Japanese in Korea during the 1592–1598 Hideyoshi or Imjin Wars, shrinking tax revenue due in part to taxes in silver being paid in weight and not by value, and inflation, all combined to create enormous fiscal pressure on the Ming state during the late 16th and early 17th century. From the 1530s onwards, huge quantities of silver had begun entering the Ming economy from the vast New World silver deposits that had been discovered in Peruvian mines. This influx of silver in return for tea, porcelain and silk, fuelled the Ming economic boom of the 16th century, filled the imperial coffers, funded both the reinforcement of the Great Wall and Ming armies fighting in Korea, but contributed to inflation.

In a period referred to by some historians as the Ming-Qing Cataclysm, drought, famine and flood ravaged the 17th-century rural population. Violence, looting and rebellion became widespread, and in April 1644 the forces of the rebel leader Li Zicheng (1605–1645) sacked Beijing. On 25 April, with all hope lost, the Chongzhen emperor (r.1628–1644) fled the Forbidden City and hung himself from a tree on nearby Coal Hill. This act ended 276 years of Ming rule.

Li Zicheng's Great Shun dynasty lasted for a mere 40 days between April and June of 1644. Rather than see China fall to Li Zicheng, a Ming general named Wu Sangui (1612–1678), in command of Ming forces in northeast China, decided to open the gates of the Great Wall at the Shanhai Pass on 27 May, letting the Manchu armies into China. The Manchu, a non-Chinese people from the northeast frontier, led by the Manchu chieftain Dorgon (1612–1650), rode through the Great Wall to restore order to China, reaching Beijing in early June. On 6 June 1644, Manchu forces entered the Forbidden City, claimed the Mandate of Heaven, and declared their own dynasty, the Qing (1644–1911), meaning 'pure'.

In terms of rulership and administration, the Qing was in many ways a direct continuity of the Ming, with the Qing adopting and continuing Ming government structures and the examination system, which suggests that the basic structures of Ming rule and administration at least, were reasonably effective and sound.

Indeed, the Ming did not entirely end in June 1644. Members of the imperial family fled south and a succession of Ming imperial descendants continued the Ming, known as the Southern Ming, until 1661, when a Manchu army finally succeeded in capturing and executing the Yongli emperor (r.1646–1662), thus bringing to an end any hope for a restoration of the Ming state. Nonetheless, resistance against the Qing continued, most notably on the island of Taiwan, but this too ended with the annexation of Taiwan in 1683, and the crushing of the rebels who had held out there.

FURTHER READING

Brook 1999; Brook 2010; Dardess 2012; Hansen 2000; Harrison-Hall 2001; He et al. 2008; Hucker 1978; Levathes 1996; Mann 2011; Mote and Twitchett 1988; Mote and Twitchett 1998; Robinson 2008; Struve 1993; Tsai 1996

CATALOGUE NO. 29

Wucai (five-colour) fish vat with aquatic decoration (1567–1572).

See page 27

Nanjing City Wall

The Ming government specified the dimensions of the bricks to be produced for the Nanjing City Wall. Bricks, such as the examples below, were fired from yellow clay at temperatures of 600–700°C.

The Wall had a perimeter of 38.6 kilometres, and featured 18 gates, along with numerous defensive features. The foundations were on stone slabs, intended to prevent undermining of the walls.

1–3

Bricks from the Nanjing City Wall

Yichun County, Jiangxi province
Earthenware with stamped inscription
(1) length 41 cm, width 19.8 cm, depth 11.4 cm
(2) length 42 cm, width 21 cm, depth 11 cm
(3) length 43.8 cm, width 21 cm, depth 11.5 cm
Hongwu reign (1368–1398)
Nanjing Museum

During the reign of the first Ming emperor, millions of bricks were produced in the provinces surrounding Nanjing. They were made for the Nanjing City Wall. (Work began on the Wall in 1366 and it took about 21 years.) Each brick was stamped with the place of production, the name of the worker who made it, and the name of his supervisors. Should a brick be discovered to be substandard, those responsible could be traced and punished.

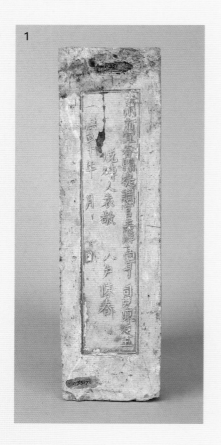

9

Architectural details and roof tiles

Roofs in historic China were decorated with protective figures, zoomorphic ornaments and motifs intended to provide protection from evil spirits or harm.

As traditional Chinese buildings were predominantly wooden, many of these ornaments were associated with water and placed on the roof to protect against fire.

Roofs were also, through use of colour, indicators of building function and of social status.

4

Tile-end in the form of a dragon

Earthenware with low-fired yellow and
green glazes
Height 16 cm, width 2 cm, depth 10 cm
Hongwu reign (1368–1398)
Nanjing Museum

In China, dragons are associated with water. This
roof ornament, like others on this page, would have
been expected to protect against fire.

5

Ridge tile in the form of a cow-headed human figure with a dragon tail

Earthenware with low-fired yellow and green
glazes
Height 16 cm, width 33 cm
Hongwu reign (1368–1398)
Nanjing Museum

This ornamental roof figure has a dragon or fish
tail.

6

Ridge-end tile in the form of a water-dragon (*chiwen*)

From the Bao'en Temple, Nanjing
Earthenware with low-fired green glaze
Height 71 cm, width 51 cm
Hongwu reign (1368–1398)
Nanjing Museum

This water-dragon (*chiwen*) ornament was placed
at either end of a roof ridge.

7

Tile-end in the form of a lion

Earthenware with low-fired yellow and
green glazes
Height 19.5 cm
Hongwu reign (1368–1398)
Nanjing Museum

Lions have a protective function in traditional
Chinese culture, and were placed in pairs outside
many Buddhist temples and official buildings.

8

Ridge tile in the form of a fish

Earthenware with low-fired green glaze
Height 27.8 cm, width 26 cm
Hongwu reign (1368–1398)
Nanjing Museum

This ornamental roof figure is of a fish, most likely
a carp.

9

Roof finial in the form of a budding lotus flower

Earthenware with low-fired green glaze
Height 39.4 cm, width 22.5 cm
Hongwu reign (1368–1398)
Nanjing Museum

This glazed roof finial is in the form of a closed
lotus bud. The lotus flower is a Buddhist symbol.

10–12

Goutou eave-end tiles with moulded dragon decoration

Earthenware with low-fired green glaze

(10) diameter 17.2 cm

(11) diameter 17.2 cm

(12) diameter 18 cm

Hongwu reign (1368–1398)

Nanjing Museum

These eave-end tiles sat at the bottom edge of a roof. As they would have been visible from the ground, they are decorated, in this case with an imperial five-clawed dragon. The yellow colour of tiles 10 and 11 was restricted to imperial buildings, and these examples were recovered from the site of the Nanjing Imperial Palace.

Tile 12 sat at the bottom edge of a roof and is decorated with an imperial five-clawed dragon. This tile was also found at the site of the Nanjing Imperial Palace, but its green colour suggests that it was from a less important building.

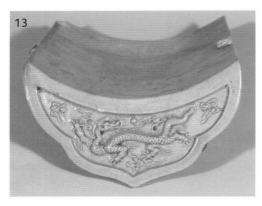

13–14

Dishui eave-end tiles with moulded dragon decoration

Earthenware with low-fired yellow glaze

(13) Length 43.8 cm, width 28.2 cm

(14) Length 15.5 cm, height 8.5 cm

Hongwu reign (1368–1398)

Length 43.8 cm, width 28.2 cm

Nanjing Museum

This type of eave-end tiles is known in Chinese as 'water-drippers'. They sat at the bottom edge of a roof between circular tiles on either side. Decorated with an imperial five-clawed dragon, they are in the yellow colour of the tiles restricted to imperial buildings.

CATALOGUE NO. 15

The Forbidden City and its architect, Kuai Xiang (1398–1481).

See page 16

15

The Forbidden City and its architect, Kuai Xiang (1398–1481)

Anonymous

Hanging scroll, ink and colours on silk

Height 183.8 cm, width 156 cm

Mid-15th century

Nanjing Museum

In 1420, Beijing's Forbidden City became home to the Ming emperors and imperial family. Below, the Forbidden City's chief architect, Kuai Xiang, stands in front of the Forbidden City near Tian'anmen (The Gate of Heavenly Peace). Behind can be seen six elephants, used for ceremonial occasions and part of the stable of elephants gifted to the Ming emperors by Burmese and Vietnamese rulers. The main palace audience halls, also behind, are placed on a central north-south axis, with ancillary buildings off to the sides.

16

Meiping (plum vase) jar with cover and floral decoration

Jingdezhen, Jiangxi province

Porcelain with underglaze copper red decoration

Height 41.6 cm

Zhengtong reign (1436–1449)

Nanjing Museum

This *meiping* jar was excavated from the tomb of Princess Ancheng (1384–1443) in March 1957, in Jiangning county, Jiangsu province. Princess Ancheng was the daughter of the Yongle emperor (r. 1402–1424).

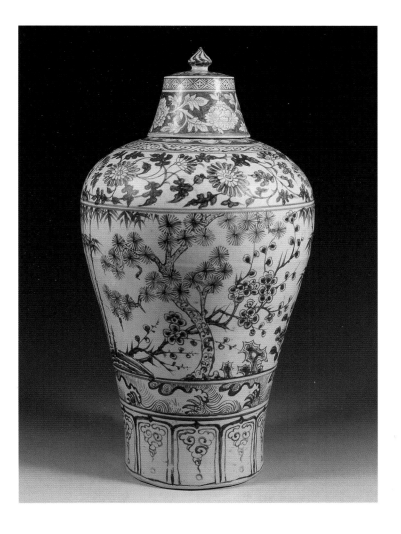

Porcelain

Porcelain is a high-fired ceramic, usually fired at 1200–1350°C. It is made from white clay or kaolin (*Gaoling tu*), china stone (*baidunzi*) and other materials to produce a hard, white, vitreous, translucent body impermeable to water. This can then be decorated in many ways with glazes, which seal the porcelain and render it impervious to dirt or staining.

The centre of Ming porcelain production was Jingdezhen, Jiangxi province. This was Ming China's – and therefore the world's – largest pre-modern industrial centre.

Three Friends of Winter

This jar is decorated with the motif of the Three Friends of Winter – pine, plum blossom and bamboo. These plants either flower or remain green during winter and thus symbolize resilience, perseverance and renewal. They also stood for the ideal qualities of a good Confucian official.

Glaze types

Pure white porcelains with transparent glazes reached the highest level of technical perfection at the Jingdezhen imperial factory kilns during the reign of the Yongle emperor (1402–1424). This glaze type was developed in accordance with the Yongle emperor's preference for the colour white, but continued to be used at the imperial court throughout the Ming.

The term 'sweet-white' may have a later designation, applied in the 16th century when the technique for producing white sugar was discovered.

The most common glaze type, however, was blue and white. Cobalt was used to paint designs onto the body of the vessel, which was then glazed and fired.

Underglaze copper red, on the other hand, was very difficult to fire with success. It was thus considered more suitable for furnishing the tombs of the élite.

17
Dish with sweet-white glaze

Jingdezhen, Jiangxi province
Porcelain with sweet-white glaze
Diameter 38.5 cm, height 7.3 cm
Xuande reign (1426–1435)
Nanjing Museum

The perfect white glaze on this dish was termed sweet-white (*tianbai*). The glaze has a soft, silky quality, somewhat like fine white jade.

18
Octagonal box with birds and phoenix

Jingdezhen, Jiangxi province
Porcelain with underglaze blue, with one hundred birds and phoenix decoration
Diameter 31.9 cm, height 16.7 cm
Jiajing mark and reign (1522–1566)
Nanjing Museum

This octagonal box is decorated with the theme of one hundred birds paying homage to the phoenix. The phoenix is regarded as the King of Birds and this decorative schema represents a ruler with lesser birds paying homage.

In Chinese, the phrase 'one hundred birds paying homage to the phoenix' (*Bai niao chao feng*) suggests a wise ruler in a time of prosperity and peace.

19

Cloisonné incense-burner (*fang-ding*)

Gilded copper alloy and polychrome
enamel inlays

Height 38 cm, length 17.6 cm, width 25.5 cm

Jingtai mark (1450–1456), 17th century

Nanjing Museum

The form and decoration of this cloisonné incense-burner is
that of an ancient bronze ritual vessel known as a *fang-ding*.
Many of the features of this incense-burner can be found in
Zhou dynasty (*ca.*1046–256 BC) bronze vessels. Cloisonné altar
and ritual offering vessels used during the Ming followed both
imperial and textual conventions that required ritual vessels
to be based on ancient bronze vessels.

This incense-burner may originally have been the center-piece
of an altar set of five offering vessels (*wugong*), including two
flower vases and two candlesticks flanking it on either side.

In China, incense came from animal
and vegetable sources that might
include cassia, artemisia, camphor,
liquorice, fennel, musk or civet. Other
aromatics, such as ambergris and
sandalwood, were also imported from
Southeast Asia.

Incense was burned in ritual contexts
as an offering and invocation, and in
domestic settings for fragrance and
the repelling of insects.

It might take the form or sticks or
cones, or could be combined with gum
and charcoal. Some substances, such
as artemisia, could be burned directly.

Cloisonné

The technique of cloisonné (from the French *cloisons* meaning cells or partitions) reached China from the Middle East during the Mongol Yuan dynasty (1279–1368).

Cloisonné involves creating a decorative pattern with wire outlines on a metal surface, and then filling them with powdered enamels; these are then fired to fuse them to the surface, and finally polished back.

20

Cloisonné tripod incense-burner

Gilded copper alloy and polychrome enamel inlays
Diameter 22.5 cm, height 16 cm
Jingtai mark and reign (1450–1456),
16th to 17th century
Nanjing Museum

The body of the vessel is decorated with four lions clenching between their teeth ribbons attached to embroidered brocade balls. They are depicted against a background of scrolling lotus and various auspicious symbols.

The legs take the form of three downward facing elephant heads. Both lions and elephants feature in Buddhist folklore and symbolism, and this incense-burner may therefore have been intended for use on a Buddhist altar.

21

Cloisonné incense-burner (*ding*)

Gilded copper alloy and polychrome
enamel inlays

Diameter 19.5cm, height 22 cm

Jingtai mark (1450–1456), 16th to 17th century

Nanjing Museum

The tripod form of this cloisonné incense-burner resembles that
of an ancient bronze ritual vessel known as a *ding*. Its two gilt
handles are in the form of single-footed dragons known as *Kui*
dragons, a common motif on ancient bronze vessels. The body
of the vessel is decorated with dragons chasing a flaming pearl
above the cresting sea waves.

Cloisonné was considered too colourful and not sufficiently elegant or fine
enough for literati taste. It was thus
favoured for use in imperial halls and
buildings, and in Buddhist temples and
other formal and religious settings
where it was used for decorative effect.

Writing in *The Essential Criteria of
Antiquities* (*Gegu Yaolun*) published in
1388, the early Ming writer Cao Zhao
(mid- to late 14th century) dismissed
cloisonné as only suitable for 'the
lady's chambers' rather than the
scholar of taste.

However, within a few decades,
cloisonné had become much more
fashionable. In an expanded edition
of *The Essential Criteria of Antiquities*
in 1459, the writer Wang Zuo (1428–
1512) noted that cloisonné '*pieces
produced for the Imperial Palace are
delicate, sparkling, and lovely*'.

22

Cloisonné dish with decoration of dragons

Cast copper alloy with polychrome enamel inlays and decoration of dragons

Diameter 45 cm, height 8 cm

16th to 17th century

Nanjing Museum

The interior of this dish is decorated with a dragon and phoenix, a combination that refers symbolically to a marital pairing, while also representing the emperor and empress. Dragon and phoenix patterns were common on the decorative arts of the Ming imperial court. The rest of the dish features colourful floral decoration with flower petals inlaid with colourful enamels in red, white, green, yellow, blue and lapis blue, standing out against the vibrant turquoise ground. The pointed petals of the lotus flowers are characteristic of the same flowers on cloisonné during the late 16th century, as are the lotus-scrolls seen on the underside with their simply rendered leaves.

This cloisonné tray features two imperial five-clawed dragons chasing a large flaming pearl at centre. Cloisonné items for the imperial court, such as this tray, were produced by the Directorate of Imperial Accoutrements (*Yuyongjian*).

Although cloisonné is thought to have been introduced into China during the Yuan dynasty (1279–1368), it only began to be produced in large quantities for the imperial court during the early to mid-Ming. As it was costly and expensive to make, its availability was largely restricted to the imperial court.

23

Cloisonné tray with decoration of dragons chasing a pearl

Cast copper alloy with polychrome enamel inlays and decoration of dragons

Diameter 57 cm, height 6.8 cm

17th century

Nanjing Museum

Reign marks

The painting of reign marks (*nianhao*) on imperial porcelain first became regular practice during the Yongle rule (1402–1424) of the early 15th century.

A reign mark typically states the name of the dynasty first, followed by the title of the emperor.

A Ming reign mark is usually six, or more rarely four, characters in length, and is typically found on the bottom of a piece of porcelain, or sometimes on the rim.

24

Bowl with dragons chasing pearls on a yellow ground

Jingdezhen, Jiangxi province
Porcelain with underglaze blue dragons on an overglaze yellow ground
Diameter 14.3 cm, height 5 cm
Longqing mark and reign (1567–1572)
Nanjing Museum

The exterior of this bowl features a pair of blue five-clawed dragons chasing flaming pearls among blue clouds on a yellow ground. The interior of the shows a five-clawed dragon roundel in underglaze blue. The bowl's interior is also slightly domed in a manner resembling a *mantou* (steamed bun).

The yellow overglaze would have been applied after the first firing of the vessel and required a second kiln firing at a comparatively low temperature of around 850–900°C.

Imperial kilns

Porcelain, a Chinese invention, has been produced at Jingdezhen since the Five Dynasties (902–979). Jingdezhen was ideally situated, with access to high quality mineral deposits, forests providing fuel for kilns, and waterways to transport porcelain to markets or imperial destinations.

Ming imperial kilns at Jingdezhen developed a range of innovative and sophisticated techniques that raised the porcelain to unparalleled levels of achievement.

Commercial kilns also produced goods for both the domestic and export markets. By the end of the Ming, Jingdezhen's commercial kilns were supplying vast quantities of blue and white ceramics to the new European market.

Chicken-fat yellow glazes

Dishes like these examples were produced at the imperial factory kilns in Jingdezhen for use at the imperial court. The yellow glaze, described as 'chicken-fat yellow' or 'tender yellow', achieved during the early to mid-Ming was of extraordinarily fine quality.

Yellow glazed wares had two uses at the imperial court. They had a function within the ritual at imperial ceremonies held at the Altar to the Earth (*Diqitan*) north-east of the Forbidden City. In addition, wares completely glazed in yellow were utilized on the tables reserved for the emperor, empress, or dowager empress.

25–27
Dishes with yellow glaze

Jingdezhen, Jiangxi province

Porcelain with monochrome yellow glaze

(25) diameter 17.6 cm, height 4 cm
Zhengde mark and reign (1506–21)

(26) diameter 18.3 cm, height 3.8 cm
Wanli mark and reign (1573–1620)

(27) diameter 17.3 cm, height 4.1 cm
Chenghua reign (1465–1487)

Nanjing Museum

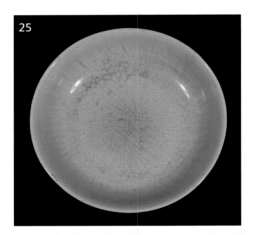

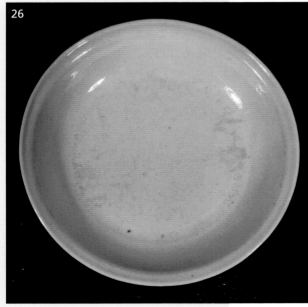

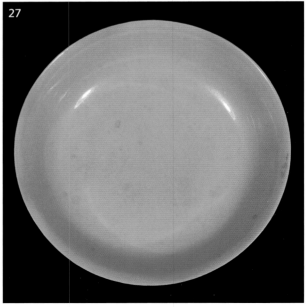

28

Bowl with yellow glaze and incised decoration

Jingdezhen, Jiangxi province

Porcelain with yellow glaze and incised under-glaze decoration of lotuses

Diameter 18.3 cm, height 7.5 cm

Wanli mark and reign (1573–1620)

Nanjing Museum (no image)

This bowl features a type of decoration known as *anhua*, which means 'secret' or 'hidden' decoration. *Anhua* designs are incised into the body of the vessel, or carved in very low relief, and it is usually only possible to observe the pattern of decoration when the object is held up to the light.

This form of decoration was typically only used on extremely thin-bodied translucent porcelains known as 'bodiless' (*tuotai*) in Chinese. The design on this bowl is one of lotus flowers.

29

Wucai (five-colour) fish vat with aquatic decoration

Jingdezhen, Jiangxi province

Porcelain with underglaze blue and overglaze polychrome decoration

Longqing mark and reign (1567–1572)

National Museums Scotland

This large vat would have been used for raising fish and aquatic plants in the imperial palace or palace gardens. Its lively and natural decoration is in keeping with its function. The large size presented a considerable challenge for successful production. Many also broke as a result of the harsh winters that occur in northern China.

30

Jar with white glaze and lotus leaf-shaped lid

Jingdezhen, Jiangxi province
Porcelain with white glaze
Height 41.5 cm
Hongwu reign (1368–1398)
Nanjing Museum

This vessel form, with its distinctive lotus leaf-shaped lid, originated in the Yuan dynasty (1279–1368) and continued in use through the reign of the first Ming emperor Hongwu. By the reign of the Yongle emperor (1402–1424) the shape had fallen out of fashion. These ceramic vessels may have originally taken their form from silver vessels of the same design, a number of which have survived from the Yuan. They were typically used to hold wine.

31

Jar decorated with flowers and plants of the four seasons

Jingdezhen, Jiangxi province
Porcelain with underglaze blue decoration of flowers and plants of the four seasons
Height 40 cm
Wanli reign (1573–1620), late 16th century
Nanjing Museum

This jar was produced at the imperial factory kilns in Jingdezhen, and would have been intended for daily use in the imperial household. The design around this jar shows the plants of the four seasons – orchid for spring, lotus for summer, chrysanthemum for autumn, and plum blossom for winter. A pattern of banana leaves recurs around the base, and cloud-shaped lappets and scrolling vines decorate the neck and shoulder of the jar.

32

Plate with floral decoration

Jingdezhen, Jiangxi province

Porcelain with underglaze red decoration of peonies and chrysanthemums

Diameter 58.3 cm, height 10.1 cm

Hongwu reign (1368–1398)

Nanjing Museum

Hongwu, the first Ming emperor, admired the colour red and decreed it greatest of all colours. Early Ming craftsmen at Jingdezhen mastered the very difficult technique of using copper oxide to produce an underglaze red. Such ceramics were therefore considered appropriate for use by the imperial household.

Underglaze red decoration tended to be used on large and heavy pieces, such as this plate. Three bands of designs can be seen. The central roundel features a design of peonies, a flower traditionally associated with wealth and rank. The surrounding band has peonies and chrysanthemums.

33

Dish with floral decoration

Jingdezhen, Jiangxi province

Porcelain with underglaze blue decoration of vines and flowers

Diameter 18.1 cm, height 3.1 cm

Jiajing reign (1522–1566)

Nanjing Museum

This dish was a product of the imperial factory kilns, and would have been intended for daily use in the imperial palaces. It is decorated with flower blossoms of peonies, chrysanthemums and camellia, enclosed within vine tendrils. The various floral designs have been carefully outlined in darker cobalt blue before the careful application of softer washes of cobalt.

Silk

Silk (*si*) is produced by caterpillars of the silk moth, known as silkworms.

The practice of raising silkworms has been around in China since the Neolithic Period (*ca.* 7000 to *ca.* 1700 BC).

Silkworms feed on mulberry leaves, and extrude silk filament to form a cocoon that can produce about 300–1000 metres of strong silk fibre which is then woven into yarn.

The main centres of Ming silk production were the cities of Nanjing, Suzhou and Hangzou. An imperial silk workshop was established at Suzhou, and an imperial brocade workshop at Nanjing.

34

Piece of silk brocade used for making dragon robes

Silk and gold brocade with pattern of *Mang* dragons on a background of clouds

Length 223.5 cm, width 137 cm

16th to 17th century

Nanjing Museum

This piece of silk brocade features two *Mang* dragons in a central quatrefoil roundel. *Mang* dragons are distinguished by having four claws, while imperial dragons have five. Only the emperor could wear robes with five-clawed dragons. Robes with *Mang* dragons, on the other hand, might be worn by empresses, imperial concubines, or members of the Ming nobility.

The robe made from this piece of brocade would have been cut so that the individual's head-opening was at centre. The heads of the dragons would be aligned on the front and back of the robe when worn.

34 [detail]

35
Silk brocade with peony decoration

Light green silk with dark green peony spray decoration

Length 36 cm, width 13 cm

Ming dynasty (1368–1644)

Nanjing Museum

This fragment of peony-decorated brocade is likely to have been a product of the official weaving workshops (*zhizaoju*) in Nanjing.

36
Silk brocade with lotus pattern

Green silk with pattern of brown lotuses

Length 35.7 cm, width 13.5 cm

Ming dynasty (1368–1644)

Nanjing Museum

This piece of lotus flower decorated brocade may also have come from the same Nanjing weaving workshops.

Nanjing weaving workshops

The Nanjing workshops were famous for *yunjin* or 'cloud brocade', a type of swivel-weave satin. The imperial court was a major consumer of textiles, and most textiles intended for the court were produced in the Jiangnan region. This area became the main centre for silk-weaving, and cities in the regions of Suzhou and Nanjing were major centres of Ming textile production.

During the early 17th century, the imperial court used over 40,000 bolts of silk a year for robes, wedding costumes, curtains, hangings and bed coverings, as well as for religious, ceremonial and many other uses. Each bolt of Ming silk varied in length between eight to 16 metres.

Designs for silks for the imperial court were organized through the Imperial Household Department (*Neiwufu*). Each textile was individually designed, checked against regulations, and inspected and approved for use before being forwarded to Nanjing for production.

35 [detail]

Lacquer

Lacquer has been produced in China since the Neolithic Period (*ca.* 7000–*ca.* 1700 BC). It has long been valued for both its decorative and protective effects.

The sap of the lacquer tree (*Toxicodendron vernicifluum*) – which is toxic in its raw state – 'dries' in a damp atmosphere, producing a hard, glossy surface that protects against heat, moisture, acids, alkalis, alcohol, salt and insects.

Lacquer is built up in layers, each taking a day or more to harden. Imperial pieces might have many hundreds of layers.

The technique can be applied to various materials including wood, bamboo, textiles, leather, metal or ceramics. It can be also decorated in many different ways – one of the most popular in China is the use of cinnabar (mercuric sulphide), which results in a rich red colour.

37

Lacquer dish with foliate rim depicting a garden setting

Carved lacquer with carved decoration of scholar in a garden setting
Diameter 35 cm
Yongle reign (1402–1424)
National Museums Scotland

This dish shows a scholar standing in the foreground surrounded by attendants bringing books, scrolls and a *qin* musical instrument. Other attendants can be seen waiting in the pavilion at left, preparing for the scholar's arrival. A large pine tree dominates the composition at centre, while three different diaper patterns are subtly used to differentiate the ground, the water and the sky.

The incorporation of diaper patterns into pictorial lacquer designs was an innovation of late 14th-century lacquer carving. The central scene is surrounded by a border containing pairs of floral blooms within each of the lobed panels. This example was likely to have been intended for use as an imperial serving dish.

39

38
Rice measure

Relief carved polychrome lacquer
Height 16.5 cm
Jiajing reign and mark (1522–1566)
National Museums Scotland

This rice measure is decorated on its slanted sides with five writhing dragons, each with five claws. The central dragon on each side is forward-facing, an innovation of the Jiajing era.

Above the dragons on two sides of the vessel is the character *wan* (abundance), and on the other two sides the character *shou* (long-life). Below are mountains and waves, while the areas around the dragons are carved with scroll-shaped *ruyi* clouds.

The measure is equivalent in volume to a Ming *dou* (about a decalitre), and is likely to have had a role in one of the numerous state rituals undertaken by the emperor. A gold-filled six-character Jiajing reign inscription is incised on the base.

39
Incense box

Carved lacquer
Diameter 11.2 cm
Yongle reign and inscription (1402–1424)
National Museums Scotland

The top of this box features a carving of a peony, while flowers of the four seasons decorate the circumference. A large number of similar lacquer boxes survive from the Ming with floral, fruit or figurative decoration. They are thought to have been used to store incense.

38

40

Wine cup in the form of an ancient *Jue* bronze vessel

Jingdezhen, Jiangxi province
Porcelain with sweet-white glaze
Height 9.3 cm
Yongle reign (1402–1424)
Nanjing Museum

The wine cup below takes the form of an ancient ritual vessel known as a *jue*, used for serving warm wine.

Used in Ming imperial rituals, the form of this vessel dates to Late Neolithic Period (*ca.* 5000–2000 BC) earthenware vessels, and to later Shang (*ca.* 1600–1046 BC) and Zhou dynasty (*ca.* 1046–256 BC) bronze vessels. This *jue*'s distinctive warm white glaze is the famous 'sweet white' (*tianbai*) (see page 18).

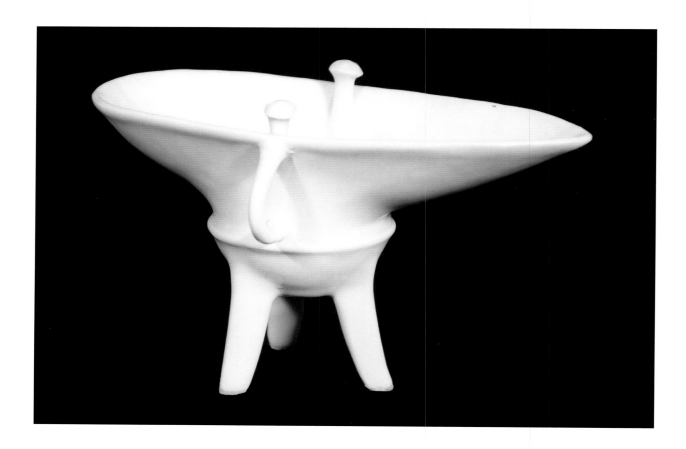

41

Jar with yellow glaze

Jingdezhen, Jiangxi province

Porcelain with yellow glaze and traces of
gold decoration

Height 31.5 cm

Hongzhi reign (1487–1505)

Nanjing Museum

This jar with glaze described as 'chicken-fat yellow'
was produced at the imperial factory kilns in
Jingdezhen for use at the imperial court (see page
26).

42

Dish with blue glaze

Jingdezhen, Jiangxi province

Porcelain with monochrome blue glaze

Diameter 57 cm, height 10.8 cm

17th century

Nanjing Museum

Beijing's Altar of Heaven (*Tiantan*) was associated
with the colour dark blue, and so a monochrome
blue dish such as this would have been used for the
imperial sacrifices held there. This colour was given
many poetic names, including 'gemstone blue' and
'celestial blue'.

The rich sapphire tone of this glaze comes from
cobalt. This type of blue glaze was perfected under
the reign of the Xuande emperor (1426–1435).

CATALOGUE NO. 47

Dish in the form of a lotus flower.

See page 47

TRADITIONS OF BELIEF IN MING CHINA

明代王朝

Three major institutional traditions of belief, liturgy and practice dominated Ming life. Known as the Three Teachings (*sanjiao*), these were Buddhism, Daoism and Confucianism, and each had its own distinct canons, sacrifices and rites, practitioners and sacred sites. These existed in addition to the grand rites and sacrifices of the official state religion, focused on the emperor as Son of Heaven and administered by the Ministry of Rites. Daoism stressed direct understanding of the nature of being. Buddhism emphasized release from worldly suffering. Confucianism advocated ethical social relationships and moral orthodoxy.

The three different belief traditions had co-existed for over a millennia before the Ming, and had influenced, and at times complemented, one another in numerous ways. During the Ming, the Three Teachings came to be widely viewed as different expressions of the same path to a better life, and ordinary people during this period engaged with the three traditions according to their needs. As a result, when Christianity came to Ming shores with European missionaries in the late 16th century, it was relatively easily accommodated alongside the belief systems of the Ming.

Outwith these three major institutional traditions lay a diverse and wide-ranging tradition of belief defying any easy explanation and often overlapping with popular Daoism, and to a lesser extent Buddhism. It consisted of a vast array of local beliefs, cults, practices, festivals and lore that constituted the varied and diffuse popular religion (*Minjian zongjiao*) of the Ming. Overall, this tradition of popular religion tended to be preoccupied with reciprocal engagement between humans and spirits, and with pragmatic outcomes, such as the prosperity of family and society. Many of its commonplace practices involved offering incense to ancestors, divination and fortune-telling, exorcising ghosts, and geomantic (*feng shui*) practices related to the locating of buildings and tombs. Its extensive pantheon of gods, ghosts and ancestors inhabited an otherworld hierarchy resembling the administration of the imperial bureaucracy, with many gods of locality, such as City Gods (*Chenghuang*) and Earth Gods (*Tudi*), occupying spiritual roles and functions analogous to county magistrates and government officials. These included domestic gods such as the Kitchen God (*Zao Jun*) and Door Gods (*Menshen*), and countless other local deities or apotheosized individuals.

Religious art

The layout and architecture of Buddhist, Confucian and Daoist temples shared many attributes and principles, reflecting the mainstream of Chinese architectural heritage from which all imperial, sacred and secular buildings were derived. Such features included an outer compound wall with enclosed courtyards within, timber-framed buildings, hipped gables (often double-hipped on larger and more prestigious buildings), and tiled roofs supported by sturdy wooden pillars.

The exteriors of Buddhist, Daoist and popular religion buildings were colourfully painted and decorated, typically in strong colours, with red being a common colour for wooden pillars, exterior woodwork and doors. In terms of spatial arrangement, and in common with imperial palaces, the main buildings and gates of Buddhist and Daoist religious complexes were typically symmetrical and aligned on a north-south axis with peripheral buildings located to the sides. Important buildings were usually placed towards the centre or rear of a monastic compound on the central axis, such as the hall housing the principal deity, with the deity normally placed facing south. Smaller halls to the side, or to the front of the building complex, would house lesser deities.

Devotional halls of large Buddhist and Daoist temples featured altar platforms dominated by individual or multiple sculpted images (which could be carved, moulded or cast) providing a focus for worship. The principal deity would be located at the centre, and on either side a retinue of the attendant deities might be situated. The scale of the images tended to correspond to the size of the institution and its financial resources, and deities might be painted and gilded, wear ornate brocade robes, be seated on thrones or within elaborately carved wooden shrines, and have canopies overhead. On the altars, in front of the main sculpted images, sets of altar vessels were placed. These included censers,

vases and candlesticks made from porcelain, bronze or cloisonné. Important halls also had colourful wall murals illustrating either Buddhist or Daoist worldviews and doctrines. In contrast, Confucian temples included very little figural art or colourful decoration. And, in general, Daoist sites and architecture tended not to be as imposing or as monumental as Buddhist architecture, and there were a greater number of Buddhist monasteries and temples.

Beyond the temple setting, Buddhism and Daoism profoundly influenced the visual arts and literature of the Ming, with religious imagery, texts and objects of all kinds permeating the daily practice of ritual and religion at every level of society. Auspicious Buddhist and Daoist motifs and iconography appeared widely on textiles, porcelain, in book illustrations, and carved or inlaid on a range of materials; depictions of popular Daoist deities and immortals, and Buddhist figures such as luohans and bodhisattvas, appeared in paintings, printed imagery, and across many media. Confucianism exerted much less influence on the visual arts, but illustrated books promoting Confucian morality became popular during the Ming.

Religion was a major focus for patronage and sponsorship, and as Buddhist and Daoist religious institutions during the Ming were significant consumers of decorative and religious arts, they received official and private sponsorship, and patronage from all levels of Ming society. The emperor, imperial court, wealthy and powerful eunuchs, officials, gentry families, merchants and many others, sponsored the founding, extension, repair or rebuilding of Buddhist and Daoist monasteries and temples.

The Sea of the Law Temple (*Fahai si*), a Buddhist temple located in Beijing's western suburbs, is an example that survives to this day. It was founded in 1439 with the sponsorship of the influential imperial eunuch Li Tong (d.1453) who served with the Yongle (r.1402–1424) and Xuande (r.1426–1435) emperors on military campaigns. He was later appointed Director of Imperial Accoutrements

(*Yuyongjian taijian*). Its murals, which also survive, were likely to have been painted by court artists working under Li Tong's supervision. In return for eunuch patronage, Buddhist monasteries offered places of retirement and burial for eunuchs, and Li Tong was interred at the Sea of the Law Temple upon his death.

The decoration and equipping of religious institutions was another area of patronage that might include the production of sculptural images, mural paintings, monastic gazetteers, ritual artefacts or bronze temple bells. Local patronage might take the form of subscription to fund the publication of a monastic gazetteer of religious texts and scriptures, or the casting of a new temple bell; many Ming monastic gazetteers – i.e. cultural and religious institutional histories of a monastery or temple, intended to enhance its prestige – list the names of those who provided sponsorship.

The development of a diversified agricultural base, and an expanding and increasingly monetized economy during the Ming, meant that more farmers, craftsmen and merchants had surplus funds available for the support and patronage of religious institutions and projects at local level.

Buddhism

Buddhism (*Fojiao*) originated in India in the 5th century BC with the historical Buddha, Shakyamuni Buddha (*ca*. 563–483 BC). It entered China during the Han dynasty (206 BC–AD 220), becoming established by the first century. It took several centuries to become fully integrated into China and for the extensive canon of Buddhist texts written in Sanskrit to be fully translated into Chinese. By the Ming, however, it had become entirely integrated into Chinese culture.

The form of Buddhism that established itself in China was Mahayana Buddhism, with its conception of numerous past, present and future Buddhas. In addition, other Buddhist beings, like bodhisattvas (*pusa*) and luohans (disciples of the historical Buddha), formed part of an extensive pantheon of Mahayana Buddhist deities and beings. Apart from Buddhas, bodhisattvas were the most popular deities in Ming China. These fully enlightened beings vow compassionately to remain in the world to help all other sentient beings achieve enlightenment. The bodhisattva ideal was a significant element of Ming Buddhism. Guanyin, the Bodhisattva of Compassion, was the most popular and appears widely in the religious and decorative arts of the Ming period.

By the Ming, Buddhism had developed into several schools and sects, flourishing throughout China at every level of society. Lay Buddhist organizations emerged, and monks provided the funerary and religious services required by Ming society.

The major schools of Buddhism during the Ming were the Chan (better known by its Japanese pronunciation '*Zen*') meaning 'meditation', Pure Land (*Jingtu*), Huayan, and Tiantai: in the syncretic Buddhism of the Ming, however, distinctions between these and other schools were not always clear-cut.

In addition, another tradition interacted with Ming Buddhism, that of Tibetan Buddhism (*Zang-chuan fojiao*), which had also been patronized by the Mongol rulers of the preceding Yuan dynasty. Tibetan Buddhism continued to be patronized by Ming emperors, and at times tribute embassies of senior Tibetan patriarchs and lamas visited the imperial court in Beijing.

Daoism

Daoism is an indigenous Chinese tradition that originated during the Warring States (475–221 BC) period. Its earliest phase, which lasted several centuries, is often described as 'philosophical Daoism'. This was essentially a naturalistic philosophy concerned with personal freedom and happiness, which saw society as a corrupting influence.

Daoism (*Daojiao*) takes its name from the term *Dao* meaning 'way' or 'road'. The *Dao* is regarded as an impersonal universal principle from which *yin* and *yang*, and all things and states, emerge, and which is impossible to define fully on a discursive basis. The origins of Daoism are linked to Laozi (traditionally dated to 604–531 BC), a possibly mythical individual said to have been in charge of the Zhou dynasty court archives and calendar. Laozi is credited with being the founder of Daoism, and the author of a canonical Daoist text, the *Daodejing,* which can be dated to the 3rd century BC. This, and the writings of another early Daoist thinker, Zhuangzi (*ca.* 4th century BC), and the later 2nd century BC text known as the *Huainanzi*, form the textual basis of philosophical Daoism.

From the time of the Han dynasty, Daoism began to develop a religious form with canonical texts, clerical hierarchies, liturgies and its own pantheon of deities. A Daoist movement known as the Celestial Masters (*Tianshi dao*), founded by the hermit Zhang Daoling (34–156), was the most influential of these, and the Celestial Masters tradition continued through the Ming to the present day.

The core of religious Daoism was meditation and ritual practice for the benefit of the spiritual and physical health of the self and the wider community. These aims of bodily, spiritual and moral perfection were personified in the role models of the numerous self-realized Perfected Beings (*Zhenren*) and fully transcendent Immortals (*Xian*) found in the Daoist pantheon.

Daoism was supported by a number of Ming emperors to varying degrees, depending on their level of interest. The first Ming emperor, Hongwu, and later, perhaps most notably, the Jiajing emperor (r. 1522–1566), were both patrons. The arts of the Jiajing reign in particular are rich with Daoist motifs and symbols.

The two main schools of Ming Daoism were the Quanzhen ('Complete Perfection') and Zhengyi ('Orthodox One'). The emphasis in the Quanzhen school was on monasticism and attaining immortality through the practices of Inner Alchemy (*Neidan shu*). The Zhengyi school, which was non-monastic, was the dominant and orthodox face of Ming Daoism; it could trace its origins back to Zhang Daoling and the Celestial Masters of the 2nd century. It was also responsible, at the behest of the Yongle emperor, for the compilation of the Daoist Canon (*Dao zang*) completed in 1445, the edition still in use today.

No reliable figures survive for the number of Daoist temples during the Ming, but they seem to have been widespread throughout the rural and urban landscape, with as many as a dozen active temples in many Ming counties. In the same way as patronage extended to Buddhist monasteries, officially recognized Daoist temples also received support from the imperial court, as well as at the local level of Ming society.

Confucianism

Confucius (550–479 BC) was a political theorist, teacher and philosopher who lived in the state of Lu (in modern-day Shandong province) during the Warring States period, a time of great social and political chaos. (He is known in Chinese as *Kongfuzi*, as '*Confucius*' is a latinization of his name originating with 17th-century European missionaries.)

After the death of Confucius, his teachings were compiled by some of his disciples into the text known as the 'Discussions and Sayings' (*Lunyu*), also known as the 'Analects'.

Central to the teaching of Confucius is the idea of ethical human relationships and moral cultivation being the foundation of social and political harmony. Other key concepts were *ren* (benevolence or humanity), *li* (ritual or propriety), *xiao* (filial piety), *yi* (righteousness), and *junzi* (the gentleman or superior person).

The texts used by Confucius for teaching became

the Confucian Classics (*Jing*). These include the *Spring and Autumn Annals* (*Chunqiu*), the *Book of Changes* (*Zhouyi* or *Yijing*), and the *Book of Documents* (*Shujing* or *Shangshu*), some of which are believed to have been edited by Confucius himself.

In the centuries after his death, Confucian ideas were developed by other philosophers and gained widespread acceptance. By the Han dynasty, they had achieved official acceptance and were adopted by the state. The writings of Confucius became central to the civil service examination system set up under the Han emperor Wudi (r.141–87 BC). During the Song dynasty (960–1279), Confucian ideas underwent a reinterpretation by the scholars Cheng Yi (1033–1137) and Zhu Xi (1130–1200), integrating Buddhist and Daoist ideas into Confucianism (*Rujia*). This reinvigoration of the Confucian tradition is known as Neo-Confucianism (*Daoxue*) and it came to dominate Chinese intellectual life in the following centuries. By 1313 Zhu Xi's interpretations of Confucian thinking became the accepted orthodoxy, forming the basis of civil service examinations from that point onwards.

A further re-thinking of Confucianism by scholar and philosopher Wang Yangming (1472–1529) took place during the Ming. Unlike the Zhu Xi Neo-Confucian tradition, which focused on textual study and the study of external things, Wang Yangming's Idealist Neo-Confucianism (*Xin xue*) was heavily influenced by Chan Buddhism and saw contemplation and inner cultivation to develop and realise one's innate and intuitive moral wisdom (*liangzhi*) as more important.

By the Ming, the writings of Confucius and his interpreters comprehensively dominated and influenced Chinese society and thought. Confucian temples (*Wenmiao* or *Kongmiao*) were located in most towns and cities of the Ming. Unlike Buddhist and Daoist temples, they did not typically have figural devotional images; and at a various points during the period, most notably and definitively in the ritual reform of 1533, imperial decrees were issued ordering the destruction of clay images of Confucius. This, however, was in an effort to return to a purer form of Confucian practice, rather than a form of persecution of Confucianism. These images were to be replaced with wooden tablets bearing his name and title.

After 1533, expressions of Confucianism at an official level were primarily textual, with Confucian texts engraved on stone *stelae* or publication of the Confucian Classics. At a popular level, images of Confucius circulated widely in woodblock printed images, particularly in the form of pictorial biographies intended for didactic purpose; and in rubbings of images of Confucius taken from stone *stelae*.

FURTHER READING

Brook 1993; Little and Eichman 2000; Lopez 1996; Mote and Twitchett 1988 and 1998; Murray 1996; Murray 2007; Murray 2009; Weidner and Berger 1994

43

Buddhist reliquary from the Hongjue Temple

Hongjue Temple, Niushou Shan, Nanjing, Jiangsu province

Gilt bronze, stone and porcelain with underglaze blue decoration

Zhengtong reign (1436–1449)

Nanjing Museum

This reliquary takes the form of a Tibetan Buddhist *stupa* (burial mound). It was excavated in 1966 from a stone chamber below the Hongjue Temple, built in the mid-15th century, south of Nanjing. The interring of Buddhist relics below Buddhist buildings fulfilled a consecratory function. The four porcelain urns around the *stupa* were used to store fragrant herbs.

The *stupa* illustrates the influence of Tibetan Buddhism on early Ming Buddhist art. Tibetan Buddhism had been the state religion of China under the Mongol rulers of the Yuan dynasty (1279–1368), and had continued to be patronized by a number of Ming emperors, most notably the Yongle emperor (r. 1402–1424).

44

Head of a Buddha

Moulded earthenware with partial low-fired yellow glaze
Height 47.3 cm, width 28 cm
Ming dynasty (1368–1644)
Nanjing Museum

This earthenware Buddha head survives from a complete standing or seated Buddha.

Large-scale ceramic figures were common in temples throughout Ming China. They were much less expensive to produce than bronze figures.

This head still retains some of the defining characteristics of a Buddha, including a raised skull bump, pendulous ear-lobes, the *urna* or dot on the forehead, and tightly coiled hair curls.

Buddhist tradition enumerates 32 major defining marks of a Buddha. Interpretation may vary according to artist, scale, medium, period and region.

45

Shrine brick with Buddha Shakyamuni in relief

Made by Song Haiquan (dates unknown)
Moulded earthenware with gilding
Height 43 cm, width 35.5 cm, depth 8.3 cm
Yongle reign (1402–1424)
Nanjing Museum

This gilded brick depicts the historical Buddha, Buddha Shakyamuni (*ca.*563–483 BC).

Here he is depicted making the Earth-Touching Gesture (*Bhumisparsha mudra*) with his right hand. This refers to the moment when the Buddha achieved enlightenment and called on the Earth to witness his enlightenment by touching the ground.

Bricks such as this were often specially produced for Buddhist buildings and pagodas. The brick is incised with the maker's name, Song Haiquan.

46

Standing Buddha

Carved yellow sandalwood with carved ivory stand
Height 25 cm
Ming dynasty (1368–1644)
Nanjing Museum

Buddha Shakyamuni is portrayed in this standing image, wearing the traditional patched robes of a Buddhist monk, the *kasaya*.

An inscription on the Buddha reads, 'Worshipped in the Hall of Heavenly Sounds'. The Hall of Heavenly Sounds was the name of the collection of the wealthy Ming merchant and art collector Xiang Yuanbian (1525–1590), who lived in Jiaxing near Hangzhou. Xiang's art collection was one of the largest and best of the late Ming.

44

46

45

47

Dish in the form of a lotus flower

Jingdezhen, Jiangxi province

Moulded porcelain with underglaze blue
decoration and Sanskrit characters

Diameter 18.9 cm, height 5.7 cm

Wanli mark and reign (1573–1620)

Nanjing Museum

This dish takes the form of a lotus flower with two radiating bands
of petals. The alternating petals on the upper band of the outer
ones are painted with Tibetan-Sanskrit characters. The interior
base roundel of the dish also features a single Tibetan-Sanskrit
character.

Buddhist motifs and forms appeared widely on Wanli-era
ceramics, and this dish reflects the influence of Tibetan Buddhism.
Arabic and Latin scripts are also in evidence, illustrating the
scale of ceramic export during the late Ming period.

Daoism

Daoism and its symbols were present throughout Ming culture, and the various traditions, schools and forms of Daoism were practised and adhered to at all levels. A great deal of Daoist belief emphasized, and was devoted to, practices promoting health and longevity, and even to achieving immortality.

The influence of Daoism on the kilns in Jingdezhen during the mid-Ming, can be seen in a dish such as the one below, right. This dates from the reign of the Hongzhi emperor who was a strong adherent to Daoism.

48
Dish decorated with Daoist Immortals

Jingdezhen, Jiangxi province
Porcelain with underglaze blue and overglaze enamel decoration of Daoist Immortals
Diameter 14.6 cm
Tianqi mark and reign (1621–1627)
National Museums Scotland

This dish shows two Daoist Immortals. At left is Lu Dongbin, holding a flywhisk, with a sword over his shoulder. Facing him is He Xiangu who holds a magic lotus flower. Lu Dongbin and He Xiangu are two of the Eight Immortals. Lu Dongbin was said to have lived during the Tang dynasty and used his sword to vanquish evil spirits. He Xiangu was rescued by Lu Dongbin, joining the Eight Immortals as their only female member.

49
Bowl with deer, pines and cranes

Jingdezhen, Jiangxi province
Bowl with underglaze blue decoration of deer, pines and cranes
Diameter 15.15 cm, height 7 cm
Hongzhi reign (1488–1505)
Nanjing Museum

The bowl below is decorated on the exterior with deer, pines and cranes, all Daoist symbols of long life. The centre of the interior shows a songbird on a branch. Kiln sand, which adhered to the glaze during firing, is evident on the foot of the bowl.

48

49

50

Wucai (five-colour) incense burner decorated with Daoist motifs

Jingdezhen, Jiangxi province

Porcelain with overglaze polychrome decoration of Daoist motifs

Height 14 cm, width 12.8 cm, depth 9 cm

Wanli reign (1573–1620), 1577

National Museums Scotland

This censer takes the shape of an archaic ritual bronze vessel known as a *fang-ding*. Its decoration features *Shoulao*, the God of Longevity, together with peaches, deer, crane and *lingzhi* fungus, all Daoist symbols.

An inscription on the front of the vessel reads: '*May the weather be favourable; may the country be prosperous, and the people at peace.*'

51

God of Literature: Wenchang

Cast iron with traces of red and gold pigment

Hongzhi reign (1488–1505), 1491

National Museums Scotland

Wenchang, the God of Literature, is a deity with Daoist origins. He played a popular role in Ming society as the god linked to examination success and literature.

Ming accounts tell of examination candidates visiting temples to Wenchang before *juren-* or *jinshi*-level examinations, in order to secure his blessing. A dedicatory inscription cast on the back of this statue dates it to 1491.

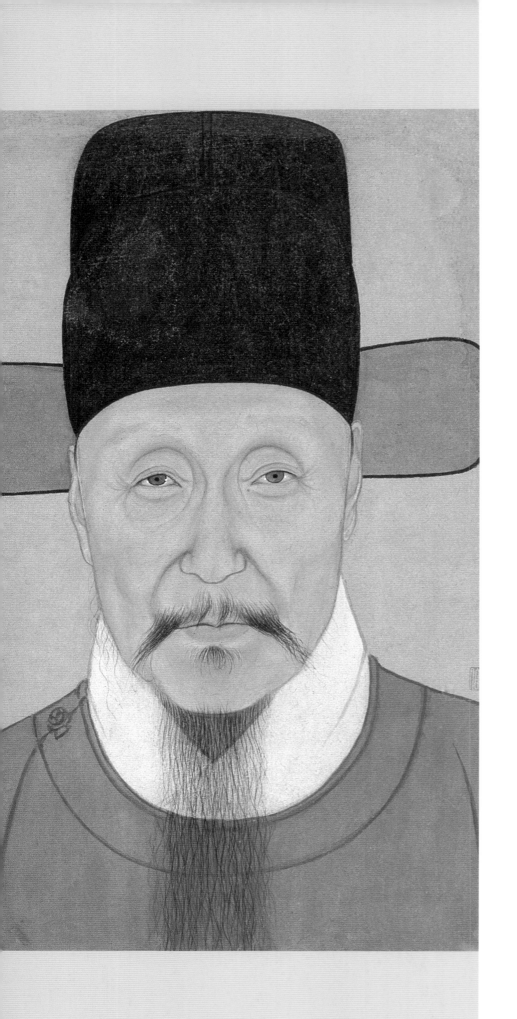

CATALOGUE NO. 55

Portrait of He Bin (dates unknown).

See pages 58–59

THE LITERATI
AND MING ÉLITE CULTURE

明
代
王
朝

The educated élite of Ming society were men who had achieved success through the civil service examination system and possessed a thorough understanding of classical and historical literature. Known variously as scholar-officials, scholars, or literati (*wenren* or *shi*), they were typically men from a gentry background who had studied for, or achieved success in, the civil service examinations (women were not eligible).

The gentry (*shenshi*) – composed mostly of rural landowners and officials who were serving, retired or dismissed – dominated Ming local society, the administration and patronage of which they informally participated in. The rural landowning gentry had greatly expanded over the Ming to form an economic, cultural and social élite which was very influential within the contexts of Ming local society. This class could afford the great investment required to provide their sons with the intensive literary education involving years and decades of study, and the books and tutors needed for examination success. By the late Ming, however, significant economic growth meant that many prominent literati and officials increasingly came instead from wealthy merchant backgrounds.

In the notional Confucian model of hierarchical traditional society, there were four categories of common people: the scholars at the top; then farmers (*nong*), as China was a largely agrarian society; artisans and craftsmen (*gong*) who made things; and finally merchants (*shang*), who did not make anything but profited from the work of others and were therefore placed at the bottom of this hierarchy. By the late Ming such distinctions not only between gentry and merchants, but between other areas of society had blurred considerably – a phenomenon noted by contemporary Ming commentators such as Gui Yougang (1506–1571) in reference to this traditional model. While this rigid and archaic system excluded many other categories of occupation in Ming society, it did serve to reinforce an idea of literati status and their place at the top of society.

The Civil Service examination system

During the reign of the first Ming emperor Hongwu (r.1368–1398), outstanding men – those of virtuous conduct and literary accomplishments – might be recommended to official posts in order to administer the new Ming empire. By the 1440s, however, doing well in the examination system had become the only route to a successful official career.

The three major degrees of the examination system were local (*shengyuan*); provincial (*juren*) – held every three years; and metropolitan (*jinshi*) – held every three years in Beijing. The exams were gruelling and the success ratio small. To become a *jinshi* was to reach the pinnacle of Ming society and status. During the Ming, only 24,878 men ever became *jinshi*, and only one candidate, named Shang Lu (1414–1486), ever ranked first in all three examinations.

A *jinshi* degree holder who placed highly in the examinations might then be appointed to mid-levels of the administration, such the prestigious Hanlin Academy, where they would serve as editors, compilers, revisers of state documents and decrees, and provide a wide range of scholarly assistance to the emperor and court. Those who placed less highly might be appointed to the central agencies and ministries of government.

The civil service examinations were based on knowledge of the Confucian Four Books and Five Classics, the legal code, Dynastic Histories, and Neo-Confucian commentaries. Knowledge of government policy and practice was also tested. The Four Books (*Sishu*) consisted of the *Analects of Confucius* (*Lunyu*) or 'Discussions and Sayings', *Mencius* (or *Mengzi*), *Great Learning* (*Daxue*), and the *Doctrine of the Mean* (*Zhongyong*), with the last two originally having been chapters of the *Book of Rites* (*Liji*) until the Song dynasty Neo-Confucian reformer Zhu Xi (1130–1200) selected them as part of the core curriculum of Confucianism. The Five Classics (*Wujing*) were texts that had supposedly been edited or compiled by Confucius, and these were the *Classics of Poetry* (*Shi*), *History* (*Shu*), *Rites* (*Li*), *Changes* (*Yi*), and the *Spring and Autumn Annals* (*Chunqiu*). These texts, and a knowledge of Chinese history, were very familiar to all who passed through the Ming schooling system, which included private lineage schools, private academies, county and prefectural schools, charity schools and Buddhist temple schools.

From the late 15th century, examination questions had to be answered in the form of a stylized essay –

the eight-legged essay (*baguwen*) of 450 characters, with each one of the eight sections serving a particular function in relation to the whole. Memorization of these texts began at an early age, and candidates for the provincial and metropolitan level examinations might typically range in age from between 20 to 45. The majority of candidates could expect to fail, and many attempted and failed the examinations repeatedly. Candidates might spend decades preparing. Indeed those who achieved success in the provincial and metropolitan examinations under the age of 20 were considered prodigies; while, at the other end of the spectrum, considerable evidence survives of men in their eighties still trying to pass the examinations.

Even if a successful candidate never gained an official post, a good result brought its own rewards, with a local level *shengyuan* degree being enough to repay a family's sacrifice and investment of resources in their son's education. In addition to the elevation in social status of the degree holder and his family, it earned the degree holder the appellation 'noble sir' (*xianggong*) as a form of address by those of lesser social status. A degree also brought with it exemption from levy labour, and commutation in the severity of legal punishments, and in some instances a modest stipend.

Over the course of the Ming, the number of degree holders grew to greatly exceed the limited number of official posts. Local level *shengyuan* degree holders numbered around 50,000 in 1500. By the end of the dynasty this had grown to half a million which, although still a tiny proportion of the overall Ming population, was enough to bring about a devaluation of the degree as a mark of status.

With a surplus of qualified men far in excess of the number of official posts available, many degree holders sought opportunity outside the fields for which they were trained and educated. Some simply abandoned the impossible challenges and odds of the examination system to find other routes to wealth and status – in farming, medicine or business, for instance. Unsuccessful examination candidates or lower degree holders might 'farm with the brush' (*bigeng*) in the 'ink slab fields' (*yantian*) as professional painters and calligraphers, tutors, playwrights, publishers, or essayists and writers, effectively forming a new professional class in the late Ming.

Degree holders who were successfully appointed to an official post came under the supervision of the Ministry of Personnel, which determined where and to what post an official was assigned based on his placing on the pass list. This in turn affected the potential for success and advancement of the appointee's career. Most officials only ever held one or two posts over the course of their working life.

There were nine basic ranks in the civil service, with each rank further divided into an upper and lower sub-rank, with ranks 1 to 3 being high; 4 to 7 middle; and 8 and 9 low.

For degree holders who did succeed in gaining an official post, the world of Ming officialdom was one coloured by corruption, abuse of power, low salaries, rivalry and feuding between various political and eunuch factions, bribery, harsh punishments, and careers ending in demotion, disaster, dismissal or humiliation; occasionally even in brutal sanguinary purges, such as those meted out by the Hongwu emperor in the late 14th century which resulted in flogging, torture, imprisonment, execution or exile for the unfortunate victims.

If an official survived all this, the normal retirement age was 70, although officials who suffered from a disability might be allowed to leave after the age of 55. Officials were entitled to a three-year term of absence to mourn the death of a parent, and such leave periods were used to escape from the pressures of official life. Other officials simply found pretexts, such as the illness of a parent, which allowed them to take sabbaticals; and for some individuals retirement was another strategy for withdrawal. The painter Wen Zhengming (1470–1559), who had attempted the civil service *juren* level examinations nine times, failing on each attempt, was recommended to the Hanlin Academy in 1523. However,

he chose to retire after only four years in 1527, repulsed by the reality of power politics encountered at court during the early years of the Jiajing reign (1522–1566). Instead he devoted himself in retirement to painting, calligraphy and poetry.

When viewed as a whole, one of the most remarkable features of the examination system was that it continued throughout the Ming to supply a self-selecting meritocratic ruling élite composed of a cadre of men with a shared set of conservative Confucian values, classical and literary knowledge, and in the process imposed on them a uniformity of cultural and linguistic identity. Yet the extensive cultural influence and reputation of the literati stemmed as much, if not more, from the artistic, literary and cultural endeavours which they pursued outside their chosen professional field.

The late Ming literati world

Those who did reach official office faced innumerable adversities including factionalism, corruption and the growth of eunuch power at the imperial court. Many sought escape from examination pressures and the vagaries of officialdom through personal cultivation which might be expressed through landscape painting, calligraphy, poetry, seal-carving, music, ink-rubbings, tea connoisseurship, garden design, or the collecting and connoisseurship of, for instance, books, swords, ink-rubbings from ancient stone *stelae*, antique bronze vessels, musical instruments, and fine Song dynasty (960–1279) ceramics or jades.

For Ming literati, calligraphy and painting were the culturally pre-eminent art forms, and the works of important painters and calligraphers from earlier dynasties were avidly collected and sought by wealthy collectors who might pay hundreds, even thousands, of ounces of silver for famous works. By the late Ming, the lower Yangzi delta region of southeast China, known as Jiangnan, was the most economically powerful and most culturally sophisticated region in

Ming China. Here, a powerful and wealthy élite epitomized the ideal of cultivated literati elegance. The Jiangnan region became home to many magnificent art collections, such as the famous collection of painting and calligraphy owned by the wealthy merchant Xiang Yuanbian (1525–1590) who lived in Jiaxing between Hangzhou and Shanghai.

At the heart of the Jiangnan region lay the wealthy and populous city of Suzhou, similar in many ways to the Paris of the Ming, such was its reputation for culture and its influence on so many aspects of Ming fashion and taste. Suzhou had recovered from the repressive measures taken against it by the Hongwu emperor (r.1368–1398) in the 14th century to become a major handicraft and commercial centre. Home to many wealthy merchants, it provided wealthy cultural patronage and a flourishing market for art and antiques. Many wealthy Suzhou merchants took an interest in literati painting and calligraphy, becoming significant art patrons who sought to emulate literati taste.

Late Ming writers wrote critically on issues of taste and appreciation, categorizing their attitudes to artefacts which were judged appropriate or not to literati taste, and in doing so disseminated knowledge to wider Ming publics which had previously only been available in the restricted circles of select literati collectors. They frequently defined things in terms of whether they were refined, elegant or distinguished (*ya*); desirable or vulgar, common and unexceptional (*su*) (which were to be avoided); and wrote widely, critically and knowledgeably on many topics. This included subjects as diverse as medicine, food and drink, tea, incense, gardens, books, paintings, furniture, calligraphy, fish and birds, plants, dress, ink, and the accoutrements of the scholar's studio.

This rich and influential literature of discrimination and taste included Gao Lian's (fl.1573–1581) *Eight Discourses on Living* (*Zunsheng Bajian*, 1591), Tu Long (1542–1605) writing in his *Desultory Remarks on Furnishing the Abode of the Retired Scholar* (*Kaopan Yushi*, 1609), Li Rihua's (1565–

1635) *Diary of the Water-Tasting Gallery* (*Weishuixuan riji*, 1609) and Wen Zhenheng's (1585–1645) *Treatise on Superfluous Things* (Zhang Wu Zhi, 1620–1627). Their writings often centred on the environments central to literati self-cultivation.

For wealthy and élite Ming literati engaged in such activity through artistic and literary endeavours, personal libraries and studios provided the physical setting for their activities, and a scholar or collector could surround themselves with objects reflecting their tastes and interests.

The essential literati accoutrements – known as the 'Four Treasures of the Scholar's Studio' (*wenfang sibao*) – were paper, inksticks and inkcakes, stones on which to grind ink, and brushes. Unusually-shaped rocks; brush and scroll pots; bamboo, wood and ivory carvings; musical instruments; fine furniture – and many other objects for use and amusement – surrounded the literati in their studios.

Reading and study naturally featured heavily in literati lives and it was not uncommon for the libraries of late Ming bibliophiles to contain many thousands of titles. European Jesuits arriving in late Ming China recorded their astonishment at the extent of literati libraries, and at the low prices of the huge numbers of woodblock printed books in circulation. This contrasted with the European libraries they were familiar with, which might only possess a few hundred expensively produced titles.

Ming literati painting and calligraphy

Early Ming painting was dominated by professional painters at the imperial courts of Nanjing and Beijing. Their large, colourful and decorative style was a revival of Song dynasty academic painting. Early and mid-Ming painters affiliated with this style were known as the Zhe school, after the southeastern province of Zhejiang. This had been home to a tradition of professional Buddhist painting and many of these painters came from there. This style of

painting, which was almost always on silk, was characterized by bold brushwork and extensive use of ink washes.

Away from the world of the imperial court, another important painting tradition developed during the mid-Ming, based on literati painting of the Yuan dynasty (1279–1368). It was known as the Wu school, after the ancient name for the region surrounding Suzhou from which its painters came. Shen Zhou (1427–1509) is considered to be its founder and responsible for reviving the Yuan tradition of literati painting exemplified by Yuan painters Zhao Mengfu (1254–1322), Wu Zhen (1280–1354), and Ni Zan (1301–1374). Wu school painting, which typically featured monochrome ink landscapes inspired by poetry and painted with calligraphic brushstrokes, became the standard for 16th-century literati painting.

The literati saw themselves as intellectual, moral and artistic exemplars, and as connoisseurs of many things. Painting and calligraphy were among the highest expressions of self-cultivation. Given their role and influence in Ming society, the art of literati painters became highly influential. Paintings and calligraphies might be gifted or exchanged with friends and acquaintances, but rarely sold.

In addition, notable paintings and calligraphies of the literati of the Ming and earlier dynasties were held in private art collections, and were typically only viewed by a few like-minded individuals at a time. These works were usually mounted as handscrolls to be viewed horizontally, or as hanging scrolls to be viewed vertically. They were typically taken out of storage, unrolled and then examined, enjoyed and discussed, and when a viewing was complete they were rolled up and placed in storage once again. Those invited to view such works tended to be individuals known to the collector, or were from the same élite peer group; only a select few ever gained this privilege.

At times, admirers or owners of such works would append their own seals and inscriptions – known as colophons – to those of the artist, on the surface of the painting, or on its borders, as a way of endorsing or denoting the cultural importance of the work. Appended seals and inscriptions, sometimes added years or centuries after a work was completed, thus become visual and cultural embellishments of a work which, when read, can reveal much about the history, ownership and responses to the work by later collectors and literati. In this way, a painting was not finished when an artist had completed it, but rather continued to evolve organically acquiring further cultural meaning and depth.

Without the demands and commissions of patrons to please, literati painters painted as they wished, according to theory and tradition, and considered themselves 'amateurs' – a central distinction in literati artistic identity – as opposed to professional painters who made a living from their work and were therefore of lower status. Literati paintings of the Ming tended to be monochrome, tended to feature expressive brushwork composed of a lexicon of dots and lines similar to those used in writing a Chinese character along with some use of ink washes, and tended to be built up from repetitive and modular elements to form the whole. A sense of Confucian restraint meant that colour did not feature heavily in Ming literati painting. In any case, colour – and with it illusionistic renderings in meticulous and carefully delineated brushwork – were associated with the work of professional painters and court.

In reality the boundaries between professional painting and the ideal of amateur literati painting, were at times less than clear-cut, and some literati painters did in fact make an income from painting. The subject matter of literati landscape work tended to be dominated by the mountains and rivers of the Jiangnan region, where many artists of the Wu school, and other literati painting traditions, lived. Landscape painting was viewed as the nonpareil of literati painting tradition, and literati painters of landscapes were not as a general rule concerned with the formal likeness or accurate representations of particular places,

but sought to convey through expressive and abbreviated brushwork the inner essence of the subject. Ming literati painting was intended to impart not only something of the inner cultivation, emotions and moral character of the painter to knowledgeable viewers, but also represented an engagement with the works of painting masters of the past.

The three arts of the brush – painting, poetry and calligraphy – were central to the cultural identity of the Ming literati élite. These were known as the Three Perfections (*san jue*) of the scholar and they found unified expression in literati painting that often combined expressive calligraphic brushwork with poetic allusion and literary reference. Hence the study and appreciation of a literati painting is sometimes referred to as 'reading a painting' (*du hua*).

Literati painting and calligraphy employed the same techniques and materials – brush and ink on paper and, less commonly, silk – and the brushwork techniques of literati painting had a strong basis in the carefully articulated dots and strokes of calligraphy. A good calligraphic hand was an essential skill for all scholars, practised and refined continuously from childhood by copying first the regular forms of Chinese characters, and then later, as the individual developed as a calligrapher, other archaic or cursives styles of writing.

In the same way that the works of noted painters were copied, the work and styles of famous calligraphers was closely studied, followed as models and collected as valued works of art. The works of past masters were copied until they had been thoroughly understood and integrated, and an artist could then begin to reinterpret the past and evolve their own style. Calligraphy retained a functional aspect in everyday writing, yet at the same time it represented the ultimate in élite literati artistic expression.

FURTHER READING

Brook 1993; Cahill 1978; Cahill 1982A; Cahill 1982B; Cahill 1994; Clunas 2004B; Dardess 2012; Elman 2013; Hearn 2008; Hegel 1981; Li and Watt 1987; McDermott 2006; Mote 1999; Mote and Twitchett 1998; Park 2012

汪生洲庚戌進士南京工尚開化人箋背原題

汪慶百字元履號生洲萬曆庚戌進士天啟初就職禮垣殺容方正絕去依阿過
大事侃侃直陳不知瞻顧會逆璫擅命家食九載堅臥不起崇禎辛未始補奉常
轉秩廷尉持衡明允多所鼂雪甲戌擢大司空未幾疏請乞嚴骨
居邑之東鄉桂岩顏其家清簡端亮素布衣正色獨立不
旁門戶生平無集字千人即朝會間未嘗問貴人一揖也周化縣志

劉憲寵號行素浙江慈谿人箋背原題

劉憲寵字抑之萬曆二十年進士授吉安府推官陞工部主事遷禮部員外郎司冊
庫往例藩府請名請封非入賄不為覆奏寵請於宗伯至夕具稿上風霜頓清
復力持代藩全嫡立庶事聲望大著時神宗儲位久虛廷臣以國本建言者皆連嚴
遣一日傳旨冊立冠婚禮官急具儀上復留中諭更期舉朝洶洶莫知所措憲寵力
請政府封還詔旨儲位定呈長孫生條上諸教誅請罷寵力
務累遷光祿少卿請告歸起右通政疏請加派以甦民困寵力
田鹽政大弊與魏忠賢忤力請致仕忠賢示東林奸黨請停加稅課皆停罷屯
餘年每有建白必依於名教一時正人多援以為重生平無他嗜好清修絕俗與寒
素諸生無異崇禎時贈工部侍郎波寧府志
按萬曆壬辰科進士履歷亦稱號行素生於嘉靖癸亥八月十七日

Portraits of Eminent Men of Zhejiang Province

Anonymous album, ink and colours on paper

Wanli reign (1573–1620),
late 16th to early 17th century

Nanjing Museum

52
Portrait of Wang Qingbai (d.1652)

Height 45.4 cm, width 26.4 cm

Wang Qingbai was born in Kaihua, Zhejiang province. He passed the *jinshi* examination in 1610, and from 1622 served in the Ministry of Rites. He was known for his '*incorruptibility, integrity and blunt-speaking. He never joined any faction or bowed to anyone in power*'.

53
Portrait of Liu Xianchong (dates unknown)

Height 45.4 cm, width 26.4 cm

Liu Xianchong was from Cixi in Zhejiang province. He passed the *jinshi* examination in 1592. During the Wanli reign he served in the Ministry of Rites. During the Chongzhen reign (1627–1644) he was Deputy Minister in the Ministry of Works. It was said of him that '*having no appetites, he led a clean life*'.

54
Portrait of Liu Boyuan (1538–1640)

Height 45.4 cm, width 26.4 cm

Liu Boyuan was also from Cixi in Zhejiang province. He became a *jinshi* in 1571 and served during the Wanli reign as an official in the Ministry of Works, one of the six service ministries of the Ming state. He later served as a Surveillance Commissioner in Jiangxi province. He gained a reputation as a skilled calligrapher and poet, and lived for a remarkable 103 years.

55
Portrait of He Bin (dates unknown)

Height 45.4 cm, width 26.4 cm

This portrait depicts He Bin who was born in Shanyin in Zhejiang province. He served as a Regional Military Commander. Little else is recorded of his life.

56
Portrait of Li Rihua (1565–1635)

Height 45.4 cm, width 26.4 cm

Li Rihua was born in Jiaxing, Zhejiang province. He became a *juren* in 1579, and a *jinshi* in 1592. He was an influential arbiter of taste who wrote extensively on collecting and the appreciation of art and antiques. Li was also an accomplished painter, and a wealthy art collector and critic who knew and associated with some of the leading art collectors and literati of the late Ming.

57
Portrait of Xu Yingdeng (mid-16th to 17th century)

Height 45.4 cm, width 26.4 cm

Xu Yingdeng was born in Cixi, Zhejiang province. He became a *jinshi* in 1601, and served as a County Magistrate in Guangdong and Jiangxi provinces. He was then appointed an Investigating Censor to Huguang province, and later rose to the rank of Censor-in-Chief.

劉伯淵琭念亭電副慈齡人一百三歲贈太僕卿箋背原題

劉伯淵字靜之父世綸生有至性十三喪母毀瘠如成人事父備盡色養敬寡嫂如母人稱長者伯淵登隆慶五年進士知泰興縣有惠政陞工部主事遷員外再遷刑部郎中擢江西兵備副使地為閩楚要衝山寇乘間竊發伯淵撫馭有方遠近倚以鎮定年五十謝病歸崇禎十年壽百歲特晉太僕少卿遣御史貴詔存問越三年始卒明士大夫登百歲者閩知府林春澤及伯淵二人而已道光亭池府志

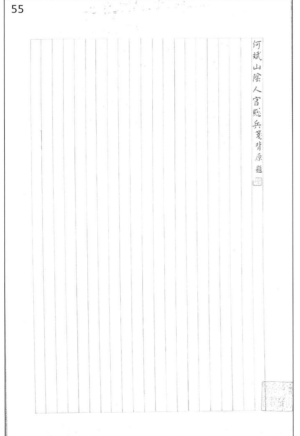

何斌山陰人官總兵箋背原題

56

李太僕箋背原題

李日華字君實嘉興人高悟端雅沉博瀟灑於書無所不讀而著述甚富工於詩

妙於書精於畫然君實之精神別有所注不欲以諸長目見於世由制科歷仕至

太僕卿浮沉仕隱家食為多於官況泊如也嘗自題畫云所著紫桃軒雜綴及畫媵諸編文雖小品目足供

熟香溫且日看其風調可想矣

蔬林幽賞姜紹書無聲詩史

先生琥九疑嘉靖戊辰三月十三日生辛卯鄉試中式壬辰成進士第三甲二

十二名歷官通政司政江西九江府推官西華知縣南禮部主事尚寶司丞太

僕寺卿見萬曆士辰歷政

右像原題只李太僕三字未詳名字里居余同時得明賢遺像四十餘幅悉出

一人手摹其間名臣忠義偏林文苑成備皆萬曆天啟崇禎三朝名賢題識箋

背或許戒不詳最簡者僅於姓名下繫一官階如此幅是也君實先生當其時

且官至太僕寺卿是必為其遺像無疑丙子秋八月吳縣潘厚謹識

57

徐煃勿直隸按院辛未進士餘姚人箋背原題

Imperial examination papers

Qing dynasty (1644–1911), Kangxi reign (1661–1722), 1670
Handscroll, ink on paper
Nanjing Museum

58
Imperial examination paper of Lui Weiqi (1635–1688)

Liu Weiqi (1635–1688), *jinshi* of 1670

59
Imperial examination paper of Guan Sanjue (dates unknown)

Guan Sanjue (dates unknown), *jinshi* of 1670

60
Imperial examination paper of Chen Tianda (dates unknown)

Chen Tianda (dates unknown), *jinshi* of 1670

61
Imperial examination paper of Guo Ang (1638–1715)

Guo Ang (1638–1715), *jinshi* of 1670

The examination paper below (and the following examples) dates from the early Qing (the Ming and Qing examination systems remained largely identical).

These Qing examination papers are for the top-level Palace Examination, success in which led to the Presented Scholar or *jinshi* degree. Every graduate was ranked by number, and each individual was graded into one of three classes of *jinshi* degree.

Exam paper 58 belongs to Liu Weiqi, a candidate from Jiangsu province, who was allocated the candidate number of 13 in the exam. Guan Sanjue, from Zhejiang province, was candidate number 14; Chen Tianda, from Fujian province, was no. 214; and Guo Ang, from Shanxi province, was allocated number 16.

Imperial examinations

Since the Sui dynasty (581–618), the examination system played an increasingly important role both in recruiting civil and military officials to government, and in creating local and national cultural élites.

After 1458 the *jinshi* degree became a requirement for the highest posts of Ming government, and for membership of the Hanlin Academy, responsible for drafting high-level official government documents.

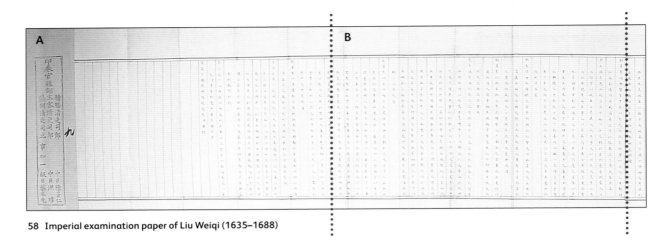

58 Imperial examination paper of Liu Weiqi (1635–1688)

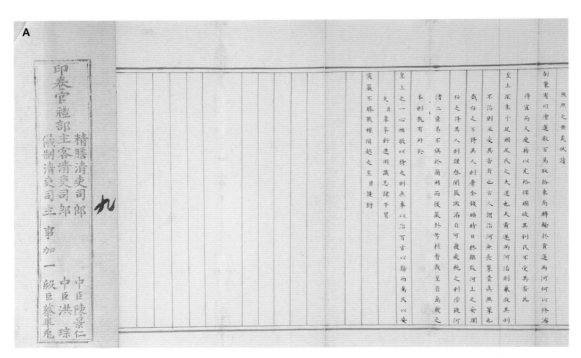

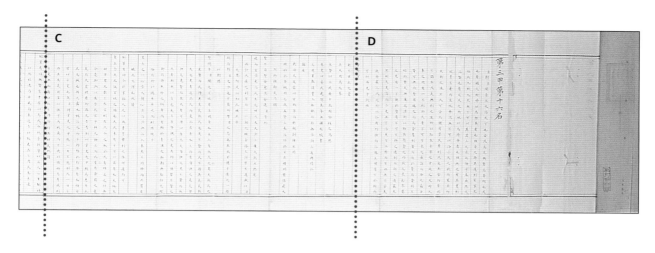

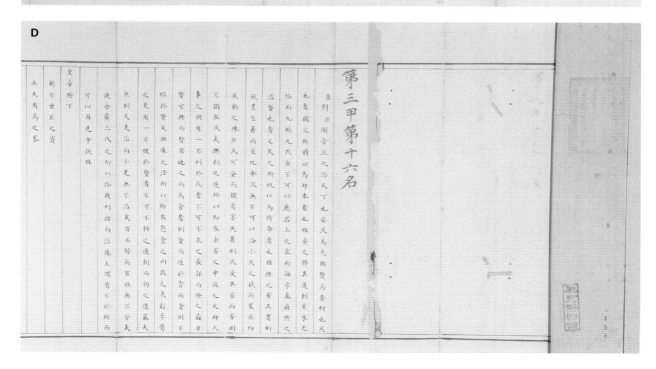

C

皇上之一心古人謂心法治法無治人未有不同條而共貫者

制策有曰今欲饒人足以成豐享樂利之休何道而可

職此之謂也伏讀

一陰一陽所以端本原之化則推視予

聖問子臣閭之百姓者至賤者也上而有牧民之吏

吏賢而民得其生矣吏不賢而民不得其生矣牧之

民之吏近於民也者也上而有撫之吏其撫之吏不賢而

撫之吏賢而牧民者可得以自見矣至於牧之吏賢不賢而

民者持無際之柄者端有類於臺諫與銓部之陛

斬而持無際則推視予

廷而咨吏治民生之理次久大法小廉之能且終歲

國計民瘼之利弊而一一詢之彫帝諮王防享有過敢以臣

聖不自聖愈求愈安進臣等於

之懿何足以知此難然乎

閭而對宜之分也不貪所擊臣之志也其敢不遜千慮之一得

以對揚

烈於繼新矢乃備

武功丕定當四宇敉寧而躬親訓練永固

國祚於金甌周已武五登三泰治功於首出穆明樂傳建大

文德覃敷值釐工科獻而甯與咨詢立達輿情於

蒲座

參吏以安民建億萬年無疆之駿業

求賢以立政庸績十五國喻穎之鴻恩

臣之藏也貢財膚所在見吾篤則以官吏之中飽為惠耳此

分意加派以屬吾民宜孚科九除三而此臺有舍箱之慶

財原有及此歲百姓不在官則在民之取於民者不可以高者也天地生

矢有民之藏也貢財膚所在見吾篤則以官吏之中飽為惠耳此

民之藏也貢財膚國之蠹也根治化而不得殊於官吏之頑安

可以少寬之歲則臣謂官吏一日不絕則民一日不

得其生是固宜以撫字為歐最而不徒以催科為考成則

官吏無所藉口而不得陰行其姦矣伏讀

D

第三甲第十六名

臣對臣聞帝王之治天下也安民為先無賢為臺何也民

也者國之所恃以為邦本者也惟安之得其道則家家先

梧而九賦九式無下不可以虞君上之求而海宇泰庭熙之

治賢也者文化承宣以為待者也惟興之有其實則

致素至善而民化承宣無下不可以洽小民之故則

民之閭有一不利於民者則民受其害而喜罔仰

不徇在民無利可安而猶有害者則民受其害而喜罔圖

集之閭有一不利之而為貪者不可不去之中故九表彭辜舉夫

賢可興而賢之法所以即在惠之內故九表彭辜舉夫

姑於賢矢興之法所以即在惠之內故九表彭辜舉夫

之吏有一不使於賢者不可不科之過剔而勁之過嚴矢

然則大夫治而小吏無不治矣百姓無不安矣

波唐虞三代之所以俗我利指而治珠上理者不於斯而

可以再見乎欵惟

皇帝陛下

躬不世出之資

其大有為之舉

59 Imperial examination paper of Guan Sanjue (dates unknown)

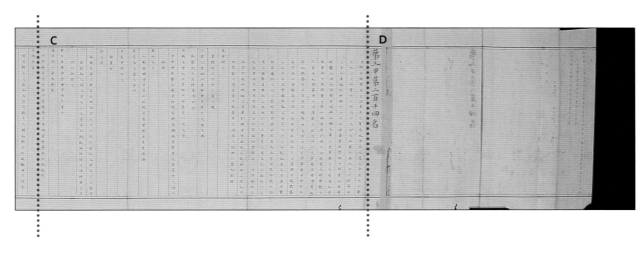

C

臣對臣聞帝王之治帝王之道為之帝王之道又帝王之心運之所運可以託天下之金而化裁於無外可以馭萬世之宮而澤施於回誠於以治化隆盛道術顯明所以託億兆民安進衆修士教誨書之救而殊無以稱夫策之惡首養之道得之德之官而治道得之教養夫而治道新三代之所以治天下之安長治者得有此是之敎養世之所共而古帝王治天下之道德下趨教養為考其所得觀是所以威之之未漠士行之不敎也為之正其本業而已古之王者�"帽民之咸所以有

西莽亦廷而垣綸之資兼絶固畏非是而致無本而然必求民德者無不明馬民德正而士習瑞女習瑞而八才出科明以正良而國等昌樂利之武備於而豊富之東見於上柳所以是而國等昌樂利之武備於

勒萁蘇訓凢所以墨民生者無不至是為民王為民俗美民俗美

茫君之尊致而作后人儀山龍

靈聦明而敬畏謀率坤平又甘之觀

勤學問而益師進振基正

聖明天子

沖平嗣服暨治與書經術定誠後誦杭育祥思馬勤等世之頌之

福淳

有道日探加之

勸農育

百道日探加之何以加兹乎

福藏百貨文教宣而民依奈天下之韶用官已人安天下之賢才晉蔚起之武之秀大小之資管已既鉄祖鲜隆之理時雍之治

進敎救以安民興賢何以安民興賢

聖不自聖圖安進具等珍

下問嚮學當王猶不是過為主皆惟草野愚臣何敢揚扡

60 Imperial examination paper of Chen Tianda (dates unknown)

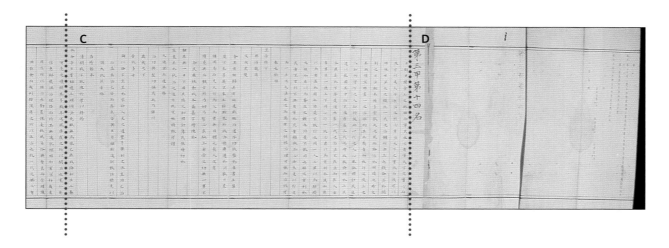

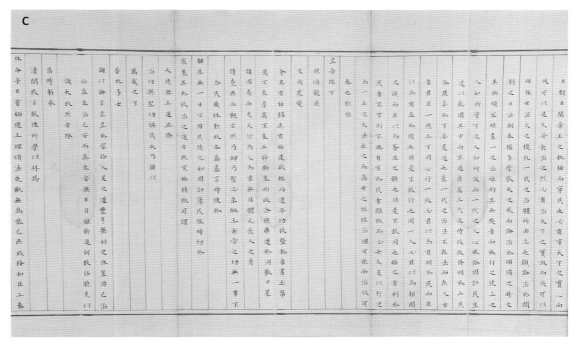

C

臣對臣聞帝王之執極而寧民也心有寧天下之實心而
後可以建至安長治之烈心有治天下之實政而後可以
昭保世滋大之模孔一代之治惟有治心也實政所由立也顧綸右於間
劃之日法制未備多崇教文之盛而海治於明備之使文
其術順宜昭盛而其無憂者無他明計民生之
是以乾隆其中而不道齊臣三代之時致教傚明私上民
人和所學下之人知所傚而的其為之名法不在法而在人古
昔君臣一德上下同心一政心以為輔國
以為有益於國也非是不敢行也用一人必
之源而臣以蒼生之顧也也推之有利於
民者不百利不與有實於民者雖治可依而治政可
為一王之大法起之為萬世之恒經治理可依而治政可
泰屯欽雖
皇帝陛下
槐頌龍愛
文成虎變
含其有壯歸是有極建威柩而道乎功致暨恭卓書王帝
與不享樂不東王綸斯章而政洛德廉運粂河散日星
謀圖易而見天於為父無非體元長人之意
續兢典而親古臣乃神乃聖心求馳王帝之功無一事下
念民慶稟和本蒞嘉言時陳哉
輸產無一日下國民隱之和國計薄民依時切於
宸衷其秋致治之方既覺精微可謂
萬歲之下
晉祝多士
治功興聖功俾茂矣乃歸以
鞠以論言皇皇敦諭人足之道豐亨樂利之休豈非已治
而益朱治已安而益求安與臣自雉新進何散任聽見以
蜀時鈐永
議大政然亨隆
昌間政不散陳所學以拜揚
清問敢下散陳所學以拜揚
休命子臣譽縮懷上理頌法克獻無為茶已應政脩和臣工奏

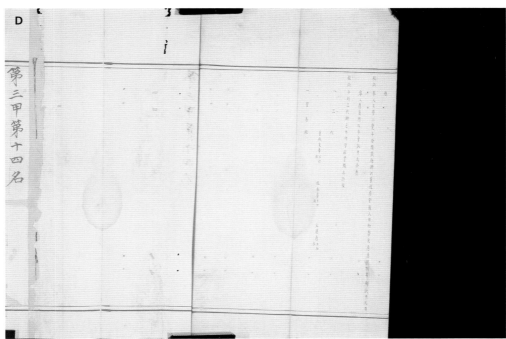

D

第三甲第十四名

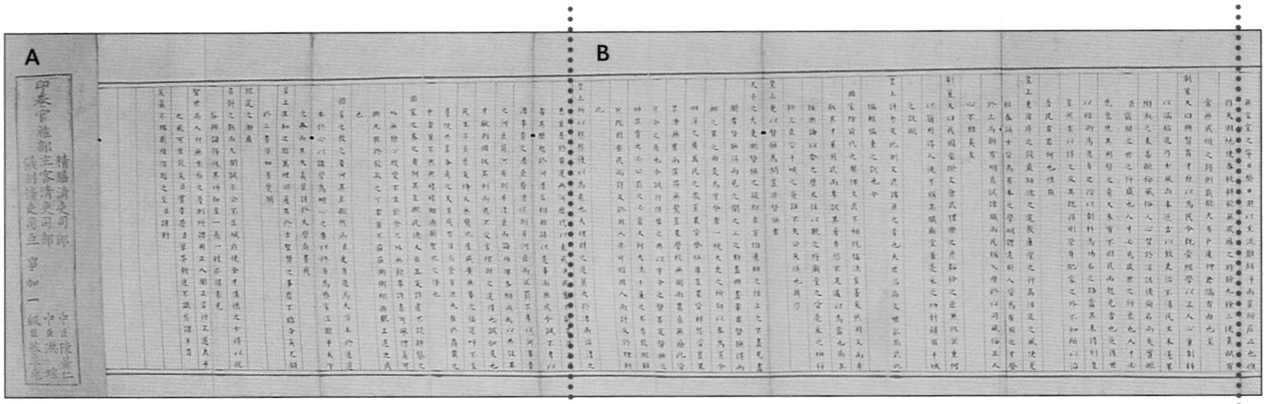

A   B

61 Imperial examination paper of Guo Ang (1638–1715)

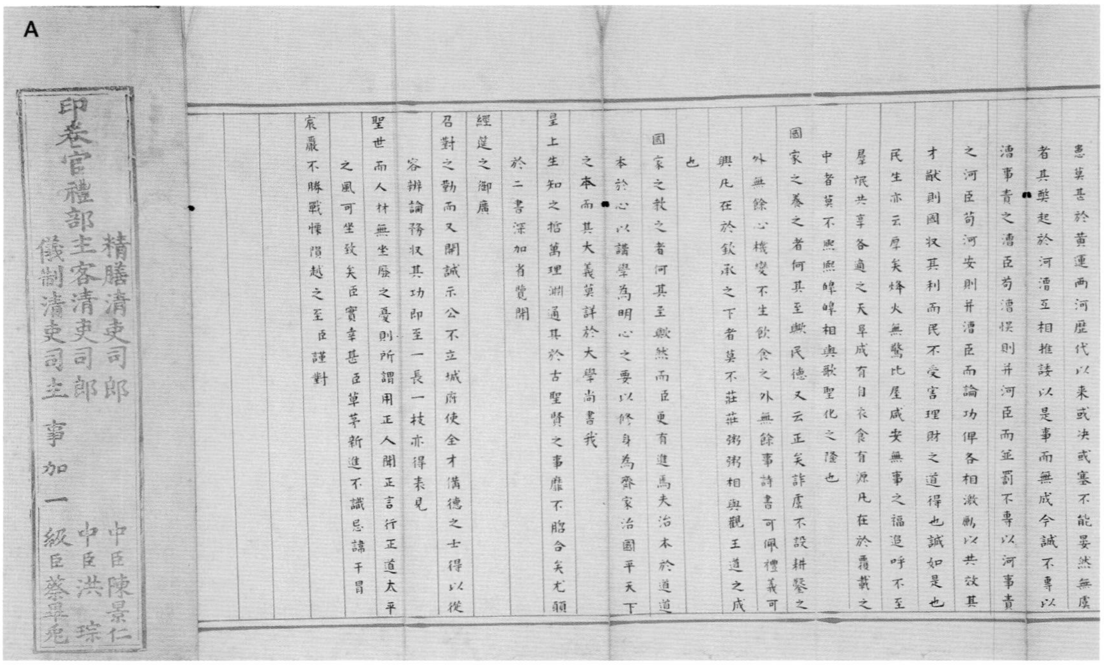

A

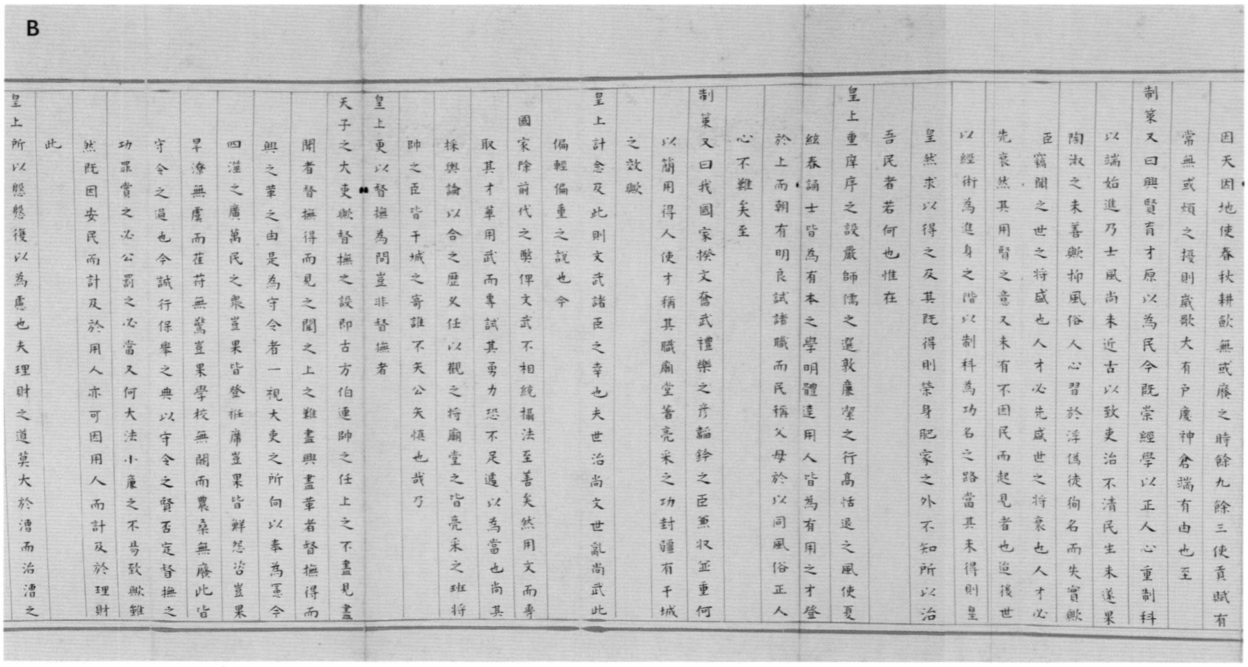

印卷官禮部主客清吏司郎
精膳清吏司郎
儀制清吏司郎中
事加一級臣蔡皐堯
中臣陳景仁
中臣洪琠

B

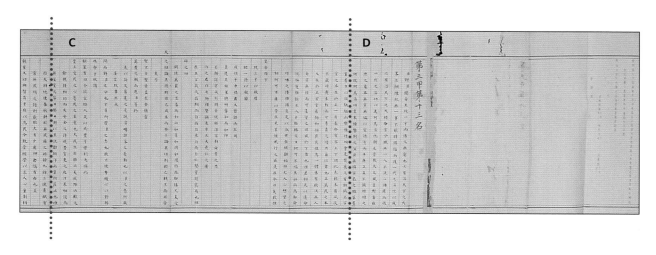

C

第三甲第十三名

皇帝陛下
統三才以凝圖
昭一德以啟眉
成位乎中惕文哲謀而互用
皇建其極軍聰明睿知而如神
至顯謨至承烈問安視膳深宮勤孝之思
作之君作之師繹繹繼通率土大堯仁之廣
應五百歲之昌期而自西自東自南自北驩聲延震辰也維
辟之功
閒德萬載之至基而如山如阜如岡如陵祚胤聯臻兄受
之詁論其德則固己咸五而登三論其功則固己軼王而並帝
萬費之服而進臣等於
聖不自聖安益求安縉富
笑乃
廷以詢及芻蕘之是誠吉嗜落之憂勤也以臣之愚何敢
妄言政事然永
問而對臣之分也不肯所學臣之志也欷不披布腹心以對揚
休命手伏讀
制策有曰今欲家給人足以成豐亨樂利之休此
皇上愛民之心憂民之至意也夫民生亦難必矣或除凶歉之
餘饑饉相仍而失安全之計或苦官吏之迫汗暴相侵而
無家室之寧日驟日圍以至流離顛沛而莫所底止也惟

業屢力以敷馳驅而樂備禮明會贊裏之有助故正百
官之本在於正一身有案上下總此克艱未有威夜
不嚴時費未勤而可專責之精共爾位者也正萬民之本
又在於正百官居師和恒臣民惝為一體未有欲沃無人
句宮無佐而可遠望之同戚於下首尚尤人心想望之
況挹運維新正人才輔緝之何可不端其好尚以造命
呼嘘之隆惟備良是以淑世在繼照始加照尤之
初何可不廣以勞求見草耀風行之盛是在今日矣欷惟

D

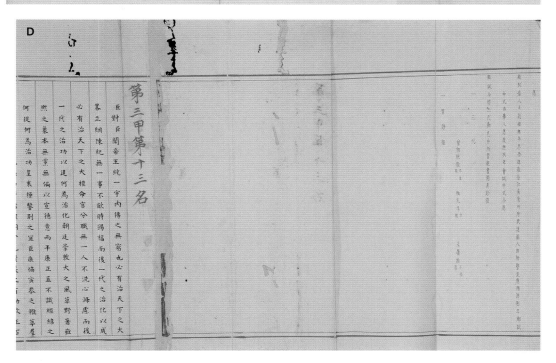

第三甲第十三名

臣對臣閒帝王統一宇內傳之無窮也必有治天下之大
業立綱陳紀無一事不欲時錫福而後一代之治化以成
必有治天下之大權命官分職無一人不洗心滌慮而後
一代之治功以建何為治化官朝廷崇大之風草野著矣
與之冪本無黨無偏以宣德意而平臺康正直不識經綸之
何從何為治功皇東操繄別之宜臣亷惝寅恭之雅羣羣

Imperial edict conferring rank and title

Handscroll, ink and seals on blue and yellow silk

Length 318.5 cm, height 29.5 cm

Chenghua reign (1465–1487), 1481

Nanjing Museum

This imperial edict was written conferring the title '*Gongren*' on two wives, surnamed Liu and Wang, of the official Qin Hong (1425–1505). This title could be used by the wives of officials of the fourth rank or higher. Qin Hong served as Right Vice Censor-in-Chief (rank 3a), one of the most senior officials in the Censorate.

The Censorate exercised great supervisory power in Ming government, and had the power to denounce officials for corruption and malfeasance. Censors were greatly feared and disliked as a result. Ming officialdom existed in nine ranks, sub-divided into 'a' and 'b' ranks.

The edict opens with four characters written vertically between two dragons, stating it is 'By Command of Heaven' (*Fengtian Gaoming*). The language remains highly formal throughout, beginning with the four-character phrase at the start of the test, stating: '*Entrusted by Heaven with the care of the Empire*' (*Fengtian Chengyun*).

Imperial edicts had the force of law and were used by the emperor to communicate orders to his officials. Communication in the opposite direction was also possible; officials issued memorials to the throne on subjects they felt required imperial attention.

A pattern of *ruyi*-shaped clouds is woven into the edict's brocade.

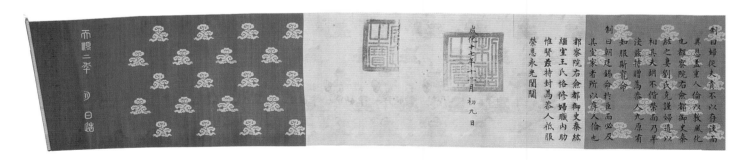

63

Dish with decoration of heron and lotus

Jingdezhen, Jiangxi province

Porcelain with underglaze blue decoration of heron and lotus

Diameter 12.4 cm, height 2.4 cm

Wanli mark and reign (1573–1620)

Nanjing Museum

This dish is decorated with a heron amid lotuses, in a mixture of pale and dark cobalt washes. This image is a rebus, or pictorial play on words, with the image of a heron among lotuses representing the ideal of a virtuous official.

The word for heron (*lu*) sounds the same as either 'path' or 'official's salary'; and lotus (*lian*) sounds like 'continuous'. Thus the image denotes wishes for a successful career.

Late Ming porcelains from Jingdezhen were increasingly decorated with figurative and narrative scenes, as well as natural motifs including birds and flowers, insects, landscapes and emblems of good fortune.

64

66

64–65

Men's hair caps

Silk gauze and gold wire with floral decoration
(64) height 9.2 cm, width 7.8 cm
(65) length 8.5 cm, width 5.5 cm (no image)
Ming dynasty (1368–1644)
Nanjing Museum

This type of cap was known as a 'hat to gather the hair' (*shufa guan*), and it was supposedly worn during the Ming to affect a look of antiquity. The forms and materials of men's hats, headgear and associated ornaments, became extraordinarily diverse during the Ming.

Fashions and tastes changed continually. The late Ming writer Gu Qiyuan (1565–1628) commented on the number of uncommon shapes and 'weird' constructions, with new forms of headgear appearing every month. Paintings and book illustrations from the Ming show men wearing a great variety.

66

An official's set of twenty jade belt plaques decorated with floral motifs

Carved nephrite jade plaques decorated with dragon and floral motifs
Each plaque between length 6.2 cm and width 16 cm
14th to 15th century
Nanjing Museum

This is a full set of 20 jade plaques for a first rank official's belt. Under the Ming system, an emperor's belt had 22 jade plaques, and officials of the first rank were entitled to 20, although this restriction appears to have been widely disregarded.

Second rank officials could have belts of rhinoceros horn; officials of the third rank were entitled to gold; the fourth rank had undecorated belts; the fifth could have silver patterned belts; the sixth and seventh ranks could have plain silver belts; and officials of the eighth and ninth ranks were entitled to bird horn belts. During the Ming, many thousands of sets of jade belt plaques were produced in the imperial workshops for the emperor to bestow on officials.

Funerary figures

These figures form part of a set of funerary figures excavated in 1978, found in the family tomb of imperial physician Zhong Lan, who died in 1495 at Baoying, north of Yangzhou.

The figures' dress reflects the type worn by ordinary people in the Yangzhou region during the late 15th century.

The custom of placing ceramic figures in tombs (common in earlier dynasties) was dying out, replaced by the burning of paper effigies of people and horses.

In order to flaunt wealth, status and power, senior Ming officials, such as Zhong Lan, did continue to commission ceramic tomb figures, although the quality was generally inferior to that of earlier dynasties.

67–71
Sedan-chair carriers

Earthenware
(67) height 16.7 cm
(68) height 17 cm
(69) height 16.2 cm
(70) height 16.7 cm
(71) height 16.7 cm
From the tomb of Zhong Lan (d.1495), Baoying County, Jiangsu province
Hongzhi reign (1488–1505), 1495
Nanjing Museum

The sedan-chair, typically carried by two or four men, was only recognized for official travel during the Yuan dynasty (1279–1368), and its use during the early to mid-Ming was a sign of status. Anyone who could afford a sedan-chair was free to use it. Restrictions did apply to the use of colour for sedan-chair curtains, with red forbidden, and green not to be used by officials below fifth rank. Ming tomb figures were commonly arranged in processions.

67   68   69   70

72

72

Funerary figure of a horse and groom

Earthenware

Height 14.2 cm

From the tomb of Zhong Lan (d.1495),
Baoying County, Jiangsu province

Hongzhi reign (1488–1505), 1495

Nanjing Museum

This horse and groom is another example from
the set of figures from the tomb of the imperial
physician Zhong Lan.

73–74

Funerary figures of servant boys

Earthenware

(74) Height 15.8 cm; (75) height 15.5 cm

From the tomb of Zhong Lan (d.1495),
Baoying County, Jiangsu province

Hongzhi reign (1488–1505), 1495

Nanjing Museum

These servant figures wear the double-hair knot
worn by serving boys during the Ming. These were
also found in Zhong Lan's family tomb.

71

73   74

75

Eight Immortals table

Huanghuali wood (Yellow Rosewood)
Height 85 cm, width 88 cm
Late 16th to 17th century
National Museums Scotland

This form of square-sided table is described in Chinese as an Eight Immortals, or Six or Four Immortals table, depending on size and how many people the table might seat.

The round legs and plain aprons of this table are a feature of late Ming furniture, which tends to be plain and undecorated. Each leg has three wing-shaped apron spandrels, and humpback-shaped stretchers below the aprons. The size and dimensions of this type of table enabled it to be used in a variety of ways in a Ming domestic setting, but they tended mainly to function as dining or gaming tables.

76

Set of four iron pictures

Forged iron with wooden frames
Height 138 cm, width 33.4 cm
17th century
National Museums Scotland

This set of four iron pictures depicts plum blossom, orchid, bamboo and chrysanthemum. In combination, these four plants are known as the Four Gentlemen and they represent the four seasons of the year. Iron pictures were intended to resemble literati paintings. When set against the whitewashed walls of a scholar's studio, they would have resembled a literati painting of black ink on paper.

77
Brush pot with openwork decoration of Daoist Immortals

Cast bronze with openwork decoration of Daoist Immortals and Dragon-shaped handles
Height 27.5 cm
15th to 16th century
National Museums Scotland

The likely use of this square bronze vessel is as a brush pot. Similar Ming-period examples survive in porcelain. Each side has a Daoist Immortal standing proud of an ogival opening above a pattern of waves, probably a reference to the Eight Immortals Crossing the Sea. According to one version of this story, they elected to make a drunken voyage across the water, possibly to visit the Queen Mother of the West.

78
Water dropper in the form of a recumbent water buffalo

Cast bronze
Length 9 cm, height 5.5 cm
17th century
National Museums Scotland

Water droppers were one of the essential desk accessories of the Ming scholar. They were used to add water to ink to thin its consistency and give it fluidity.

Ming society was primarily agrarian, and water buffalos, which were used for ploughing and farm work, were of great importance. The water buffalo or ox was also associated with the arrival of Spring, fertility and productivity.

79
Lacquer brush handle and cover with design of peonies

Relief carved lacquer with peony decoration and animal hair
Length 24.8 cm
15th to 16th century
National Museums Scotland
(no image)

Ming period lacquer brush handles are typically tubular and straight. The brush was the primary tool of the Ming scholar, and the finely carved lacquer brush featured in this exhibition is a luxury item, given both the expense of lacquer work and the skill of carving evident in the decoration of peonies on the handle.

It is likely to have been produced in one of the many lacquer work-shops established in Fujian province during the mid- to late Ming. Peonies are associated with Spring, and are symbolic of rank and wealth.

77

78

Zhu Yunming

Calligraphy in cursive grass script

By Zhu Yunming (1460–1527)
Hanging scroll, ink on paper
Height 149.8 cm, width 51.5 cm
Late 15th to early 16th century
Nanjing Museum

Zhu Yunming was renowned for his wild-cursive calligraphy, of which this is an example, which he concentrated on developing in his later years. His style follows that of the famous Tang dynasty (618–907) calligraphers Huai Su (739–799) and Zhang Xu (*ca.*700–750), both known for their bold and wildly expressive work.

Born into a wealthy Suzhou family, Zhu Yunming was a leading figure among the painters and calligraphers of the Wu school, counting Wen Zhengming (1470–1559) and Tang Yin (1470–1524) among his peers.

However, he repeatedly failed the civil service examinations, and lived a drunken and dissolute life, visiting brothels and playing an ancient form of chess.

At the age of 54, Zhu Yunming was recommended to an appointment as a county magistrate in Guangdong, where he served for five years until 1521, after which he retired to engage in literary and artistic pursuits.

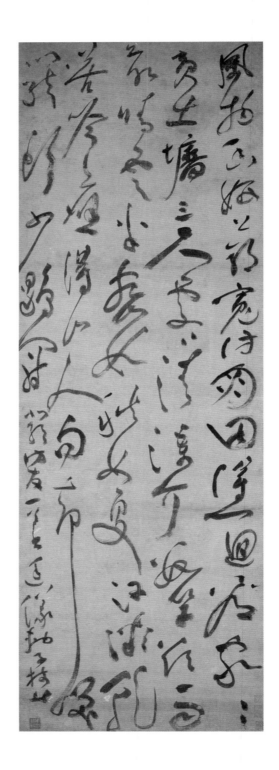

81

Stormy waves on Dongting Lake

By Yuan Shangtong (1570–*ca*.1661)
Hanging scroll, ink and colours on paper
Height 174 cm, width 95.3 cm
Late 15th to 16th century
Nanjing Museum

Yuan Shantong

In his figurative work, the Suzhou painter Yuan Shangtong often depicted ordinary people.

He was noted for his expressive and spirited brushwork, evoking the representational traditions of the Five Dynasties (902–979) and Song dynasty (960–1279) painting.

In this painting, sailors on two ships frantically attempt to prevent their vessels from being broken against the rocks by surging storm waves. The animation of the boatmen and the waves is in contrast to the tense still-ness of the onlookers in the shore-side pavilion gazing out at the struggles of the boatmen.

Dongting Lake is situated in Hunan province, and is China's second largest lake.

Dong Qichang

This calligraphic verse is by Dong Qichang, a towering figure in late Ming painting and a hugely influential painter, calligrapher, art collector, connoisseur and critic.

Dong Qichang's theories and writings on the history of Chinese painting up to the late Ming, have exerted great influence on the country's art history. His judgements, categorizations and groupings of painters of the Ming and earlier dynasties, have exerted a profound and determining effect on the subject.

Dong Qichang gained his *jinshi* in 1589, and served periodically in official positions, some at ministerial level. He only served for brief periods, alternating with longer periods of retirement, and he finally left at the age of 79.

This verse, in cursive script, celebrates the arrival of a friend from his home, the then small town of Shanghai.

82

Curtailed five-character quatrain in cursive grass script

By Dong Qichang (1555–1636)
Hanging scroll, ink on silk
Height 154.5 cm, width 54 cm
16th to 17th century
Nanjing Museum

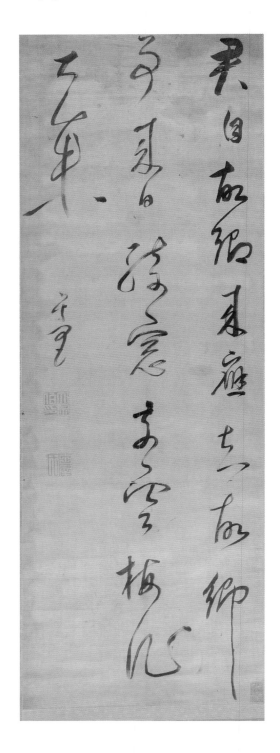

83

Small island with colourful birds and lotuses

By Zhou Zhimian (*ca*.1550–*ca*.1610)

Hanging scroll, ink and colours on silk

Height 93 cm, width 47 cm

Late 16th century

Nanjing Museum

Zhou Zhimian

Born in Suzhou, Zhou Zhimian was known for the life-like nature of his bird-and-flower painting, of which this is an example.

Little is known about his life, and even his dates are uncertain. It is thought that he attained the *juren* degree sometime during the mid-16th century.

The pair of mandarin ducks that feature in this painting are a standard symbol for marital bliss – the species is believed to mate for life. The lotus flowers and kingfisher overarch, framing the composition, with the ducks at centre, imparting a sense of elegant movement overall. This is very characteristic of Zhou Zhimian's work.

Li Liufang

Born in Jiading, near Shanghai, Li Liufang gained his *juren* degree in 1606, aged 33, but never succeeded in gaining a *jinshi*.

In terms of painting, he was much influenced by the Yuan dynasty literati painters Wu Zhen (1280–1354) and Huang Gongwang (1269–1354), and this painting is suggestive of Wu Zhen's work in particular.

Li Liufang was later grouped among the Four Masters of Jiading, and the Nine Friends of Painting, which also included Dong Qichang.

Pavilion in an autumn grove

By Li Liufang (1575–1629)
Hanging scroll, ink on paper
Height 122 cm, width 40.2 cm
Late 16th to early 17th century
Nanjing Museum

85

Pine, rock and daylily blossom

By Chen Chun (1483–1544)
Hanging scroll, ink and colours on paper
Early 16th century
Nanjing Museum

Chen Chun

Chen Chun studied under Wen Zhengming, one of the masters of the Wu school, although his paintings were very different.

In his landscapes, Chen Chun developed a much more free style. He was particularly known for his bird-and-flower paintings.

The pines, daylilies and the *lingzhi* fungus at the base of the rock in this painting, are all associated with longevity and may have been a gift expressing that wish to the recipient.

86

Painting table

Huanghuali wood (Yellow Rosewood)
with a tieli wood (Ironwood) top

Height 82.3 cm, length 143 cm,
width 75.1 cm

Wanli reign (1573–1620), 1595

Nanjing Museum

Fine painting tables were much prized by Ming scholar-artists, who used them for writing, painting and calligraphy. Some even inscribed their tables extolling their virtues.

A laudatory inscription near the top of one of the legs reads: *'The material is beautiful but durable, and the craftsmanship is pure but graceful. I will lean on you and you will comfort me for a hundred years. Inscribed by Old Chong Yan on New Year's Day of the 23rd year of the Wanli reign (1595).'*

This type of table form can be traced back to the Song dynasty (960–1279). In keeping with the best Ming furniture, it employs a design of spare simplicity, elegantly pleasing proportions and refined durability.

87

Bamboo brush pot depicting a scholar writing

Attributed to Zhu Sansong (late 16th to
early 17th century)

Carved bamboo

Height 16.4 cm, diameter 12 cm

Late 16th to early 17th century

Nanjing Museum

The openwork carving on this brush pot shows a scholar preparing to write, while a servant by his side grinds ink. Another servant can be seen heating wine. The scene refers to a line in a poem by the famed Tang dynasty (618–907) poet, Bai Juyi (772–846).

This bamboo brush pot, carved by Zhu He, is the kind of object associated with the taste of the Ming literati élite. Three members of the Zhu family were leading craftsmen in the Jiading School of bamboo carving, located near present-day Shanghai.

The brush pot is inscribed '*Old Man of the Qin inscribes this fine object made by Zhu He*' and '*Treasure of the Hall of the Three Pines*'. This refers to the well-known Jiading bamboo carver Zhu Sansong (late 16th to early 17th century), a descendant of Zhu He.

Bamboo

Bamboo was held in esteem by Ming literati. It exemplified unyielding integrity, modesty and nobility – all admirable literati qualities.

The Jiangnan region was the cultural heartland of Ming literati, and a major centre for bamboo carving developed there.

88

87

88

Bamboo brush pot carved with pines and cranes

Carved by Zhu He (unknown dates)
Carved bamboo
Height 17.8 cm, diameter 14.9 cm by 8.9 cm
Early to mid-16th century
Nanjing Museum

This brush pot was commissioned as an eightieth birthday gift for a Mr Fu Xibo. It shows cranes amid pine trees, both symbols of longevity, making it highly appropriate as a birthday gift. The extraordinarily skilful high-relief work on this piece is one of the finest surviving examples of Zhu family carving. Carved by Zhu He, this is the kind of object associated with the taste of Ming literati élite. Three members of the Zhu family were leading carvers in the Jiading School of bamboo carving, located near present-day Shanghai.

89

Bamboo brush pot depicting the Seven Sages of the Bamboo Grove

Carved bamboo
Height 14.1 cm, diameter 13.5 cm
15th to 16th century
Nanjing Museum

The scene around this brush pot shows seven men seated in a bamboo grove. A servant at left prepares warmed wine, while a second servant, at right, pours wine for one of the scholars. These are the Seven Sages of the Bamboo Grove, a group of scholars, artists, musicians and poets interested in Daoism, who lived during the 3rd century. They opted out of official life to live in the countryside indulging their interests in drinking, and in intellectual and artistic pursuits. This became a very popular theme in painting and decorative arts of the Ming.

90

Bamboo brush pot depicting scholars amid bamboo groves

Carved bamboo with lacquered interior
Height 18.6 cm, diameter 15.5 cm
Ming dynasty (1368–1644)
Nanjing Museum

In the focal scene on this brush pot, a group of scholars cluster around a table, engaged in the key signifying activities of the scholarly élite – writing verse and reading texts.

Above them, another group of scholars plays *weiqi* (Go). They are in a mountain setting surrounded by bamboo groves and *wutong* trees, with a band of clouds above, encircling the rim of the brush pot.

Scenes such as this, of scholars at leisure in a literary gathering or engaged in cultural pursuits, were abundant in the visual and decorative arts of the Ming.

91

Fisherman

Carved bamboo root
Height 16.2 cm, diameter 12.5 cm
16th to 17th century
Nanjing Museum

This carving shows a fisherman pulling fish from an openwork basket. The material used, and the subject matter, reflect Ming literati taste, which tended to favour highly naturalistic and often humorous figurative carvings.

89

90

91

Zhao Zuo

Zhao Zuo was born in Songjiang, part of present-day Shanghai, and lived there in poverty all his life. Usually associated with the Yunjian School, he was one of a number of painting cliques that flourished in the late Ming Jiangnan region.

His landscapes are particularly well known. These were painted in a manner evoking the traditions of the Five Dynasties (902–979) painter Dong Yuan (*ca.*934–962), and the Yuan dynasty (1279–1368) painter Huang Gongwang (1269–1354).

Zhao Zuo was a contemporary and a close friend of the leading late Ming painter and theorist Dong Qichang (1555–1636); their painting styles are similar. When Dong Qichang was overwhelmed with demands for his own paintings to repay obligations, he frequently asked Zhao Zuo to paint for him as a 'substitute brush', and then put his own signature to the work.

92
Boating amid streams and mountains

By Zhao Zuo (*ca.*1570–*ca.*1633)
Hanging scroll, ink and colours on silk
Early 17th century
Nanjing Museum

93
Flock of birds in an old tree

By Yuan Shangtong (1570–*ca*.1661)
Hanging scroll, ink on paper
Late 15th to 16th century
Nanjing Museum

Yuan Shangtong

This lively painting by the Suzhou painter Yuan Shangtong shows seven jackdaws clustered around the withered branch of an old tree shaped like a curved bow.

Using bold brushwork, the artist depicts each of the seven jackdaws with different attitudes, imbuing each with a distinctive character.

Yuan Shangtong was known to paint bird-and-flower, figurative and land-scape paintings. He was also noted for his expressive and spirited brush-work, which evoked representational traditions in Song dynasty (960–1279) painting.

Tang Yin

Tang Yin was a gifted and accomplished painter, readily able to turn his brush to landscapes, genre or narrative subjects.

He was born the son of a restaurant owner in Suzhou and acclaimed as one of the Four Masters of Ming painting, along with Wen Zhengming (1470–1559), Shen Zhou (1427–1509), and Qiu Ying (*ca.*1495–1552).

An extraordinarily gifted painter, dramatist and writer, Tang Yin gained the *juren* degree in 1498, achieving first place.

While in Beijing for the 1499 *jinshi* examinations, Tang Yin was caught up in a cheating scandal and was imprisoned, tortured and banned from taking the exams. Unable to progress in official life, he gave himself over to a life of pleasure, drunkenness and poverty and was forced to make a living as a professional painter.

In the painting on this page, Tang Yin elegantly evokes in a moment a musical reflection. The musician or courtesan of the painting plays a jade flute, and the delicate and sumptuous textures of her silk robes, ribbons and kingfisher headdress have been fluidly and meticulous brought to life.

94
Lady playing a bamboo flute

By Tang Yin (1470–1524)
Hanging scroll, ink and colours on paper
Height 164.8 cm, width 89.5 cm
Zhengde reign (1506–1521), 1520
Nanjing Museum

Tang Yin

95

Ancient trees and secluded bamboo grove

By Tang Yin (1470–1524)

Hanging scroll, ink on silk

Height 146 cm, width 148.2 cm

Late 15th to early 16th century

Nanjing Museum

This landscape demonstrates Tang Yin's interest in the Song dynasty (960–1279) painting traditions of Li Cheng (919–967), Guo Xi (*ca.* 1020–*ca.* 1090) and Li Tang (*ca.* 1050–1130) through its use of brushstrokes, subject matter and composition. It shows his great technical mastery of ink tonalities and of brushwork through the use of textured 'axe-cut' strokes.

Jade

Jade has always been especially valued in Chinese culture for its toughness, colour, texture, translucence and tactile qualities.

It has many associations in China, with Confucius (551–479 BC) famously having likened its qualities to the most noble human virtues.

The English term jade (*yu*) refers to two groups of silicate minerals – nephrite and jadeite. Ming jade is nephrite and the main source of Ming jade, in what is now known as Xinjiang province, lay beyond the Ming's northwest borders. Suzhou was the leading centre of Ming jade carving, with Yangzhou likewise important.

In earlier dynasties, jade objects often had a ritual or ceremonial function, but by the Ming most jade was for decorative use.

Jade can range in colour from white to black, with red, browns and greens being commonplace. One of the most prized jade colours during the Ming was the famed mutton-fat jade (*yangzhi yu*), with its marbled white or yellowish colour.

96–97
Jade *bi* discs

Carved nephrite

(96) Zhou dynasty (1046–256 BC),
7th to 5th century BC (no image)

(97) Eastern Zhou dynasty (771–221 BC) to
Han dynasty (206 BC–AD 220)

National Museums Scotland

Circular jade discs were one of the mostly commonly found forms in ancient Chinese jade carving. Discs such as the one below were used as gifts, offerings and sacrifices during the Zhou dynasty (1046–256 BC) and in earlier periods. They were also enclosed in burials to ornament the dead. *Bi* discs could be carved with patterns, or left uncarved and highly polished.

Bi discs have been a feature of early Chinese culture since the Neolithic Period (*ca*.7000–*ca*.1700 BC), but have appeared in some early Chinese cultures and dynastic periods with greater frequency than in others. Their functions may also have varied, but they appear to have been used as ceremonial items and to have served as symbols of rank. They also became an essential feature of élite burial practice during the Zhou and Han dynasties.

97

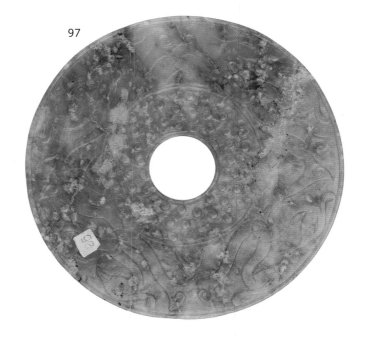

98

Bronze ritual food vessel (*ding*)

Cast bronze with stylized animal masks

Height 22.5 cm

Late Shang dynasty (*ca.*1600–1046 BC);
early Western Zhou dynasty (1046–771 BC)

National Museums Scotland

This tripod bronze vessel, known as a *ding*, is a food vessel, for use in state rituals, and élite clan and family ceremonies to the ancestors. *Ding* vessels are one of the most common surviving bronze vessels from the Shang and Zhou dynasties. The vessel below features a design of cicadas around the body. It would have been one of a larger set of bronze banqueting vessels.

Bronze

In addition to its use in rituals and ceremonies, bronze vessels were also enclosed in burials during the Shang and Zhou dynasties, for use by their owners in the afterlife. Number and size of vessels were typical indicators of rank.

During the Song dynasty (960–1279), and continuing into the Ming, scholars and emperors developed a great interest in collecting ancient bronze vessels. Rediscovered bronzes vessels were greatly valued for their connection to antiquity, as well as for such physical qualities as their patination.

99

Bronze ritual wine beaker (*gu*)

Cast bronze with stylized animal masks
Height 22.5 cm
Late Shang dynasty (*ca.*1600–1046 BC)
National Museums Scotland

This distinctively trumpet-shaped bronze vessel, known as a *gu*, was used for wine-drinking in rituals and ceremonies. Wine-drinking formed a significant element of ceremonies to the ancestors during the Shang dynasty and this vessel form was popular at that time.

100

Bronze ritual food vessel (*fang gui*)

Cast bronze with stylized animal masks and dragon-shaped handles
Early Western Zhou dynasty (1046–771 BC), with later inscription
National Museums Scotland

This bronze vessel, known as a *fang gui*, is a food offering vessel for use in state rituals and family ceremonies to the ancestors. It would have been one of a larger set of bronze banqueting vessels used for food and drink. The body of the vessel features an animal mask design common to an ancient bronze vessel known as a *taotie*.

101

Bronze ritual food vessel (*gui*)

Cast bronze with stylized animal masks and animal-shaped handles
Early Western Zhou dynasty (1046–771 BC)
National Museums Scotland

This circular bronze vessel is for food offerings. Known as a *gui*, it formed part of a larger set of bronze banqueting vessels.

102

102

Gold cicada on a leaf of jade

Carved jade and gold
Cicada length 2 cm, leaf length 5.2 cm
Late 15th to early 16th century
Nanjing Museum

This gold cicada was excavated from the family tombs of an official named Zhang Anwan at Wufeng Mountain in Wu County, Jiangsu province, in 1954. The workmanship of both the cicada and leaf are flawless.

In Classical Chinese, a play on words for the phrase 'golden cicada on a jade leaf' (*Jinchan Yuye*) sounds like a compliment to a woman for her unsurpassed beauty.

A wide range of sophisticated goldsmithing techniques, including filigree, granulation, inlaying, punching, embossing, chasing and ring-matting, seem to have become prevalent in China following the introduction of Islamic and Central Asian gold-working traditions during the Mongol Yuan dynasty (1279–1368).

103–104

Two pairs of gold earrings ('ear-drops')

From a tomb in Daqiangmen, Wuxi, Jiangsu province
(103) gold; length 4.6 cm
(104) gold with filigree; length 7 cm
Ming dynasty (1368–1644)
Nanjing Museum (no images)

Golden earrings were known as 'ear-drops' (*erzhui*) during the Ming. The ear-drops (103) take the form of two boys holding lotus stems, a popular motif during the Ming It was a rebus or visual pun interpreted in a number of ways, but its usual meaning was continual happiness, success or many children. The other ear-drops (104) are in the shape of a double-gourd, a popular Daoist motif, associated with protective qualities.

Ding ware

The *Ding* kilns developed the technique of upside-down firing which improved the efficiency of the kiln's capacity, meaning greater mass-production.

Ding bowls were stacked in the kiln with the unglazed mouth-rims resting on unglazed props. After firing, the rough mouth-rims were bound with copper rings.

Jun ware

Ming connoisseurs referred to Jun ware as one of the Five Great Wares (*Wu da yao*) of the Song dynasty (960–1279). Along with *Ding*, *Ru*, *Guan* and *Ge* wares, they were much prized and sought after.

Jun's opalescent glaze was greatly admired by collectors and remains one of the most complex of Chinese glazes, both in structure and appearance.

Production of *Jun* wares began during the Northern Song (960–1127) and continued through the Ming Period.

105

Ding ware dish with floral decoration

Ding kilns, Hebei province

Glazed stoneware with underglaze relief floral decoration and copper rim

Diameter 13 cm

Song dynasty (960–1279), 12th to 13th century

National Museums Scotland

This dish is characteristic of the famed Song dynasty *Ding* ware – one of the Five Classic ceramic wares of the Song. It features a low relief underglaze moulded decoration of peonies surrounded by scrolling and geometric borders. The warm creamy ivory tones of the glaze colour are another distinctive feature of *Ding* ware.

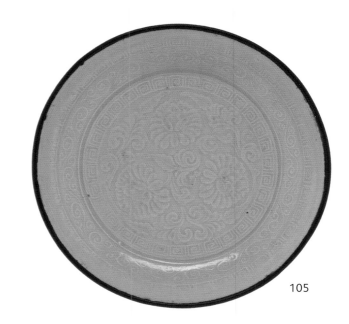

105

106

107

106

Jun ware *jardinière* basin

Jun kilns, Henan province

Glazed stoneware

Length 18 cm, height 5.3 cm, width 14.3 cm

Song dynasty (960–1279) or Jin dynasty
(1115–1234), 12th to 13th century

National Museums Scotland

This *Jun* ware *jardinière* was made as a basin for
a matching flower-pot and originally would have
only been complete when paired together. Ming
paintings of scholar's gardens show *Jun* basins like
this being used for bonsai (*penjing*) or narcissus
bulbs. Some Ming scholars also used them as
brush-washers. The complexity of the moulded
form, and 'earthworm tracks' or wandering lines
seen in the glaze on the interior of the basin, are
both characteristic of *Jun* ware. The basin features
a quadri-lobed rim and *ruyi*-shaped feet at each
corner.

107

Jun ware bowl

Jun kilns, Henan province

Glazed stoneware

Height 9 cm, diameter 15 cm

Song dynasty (960–1279) or Jin dynasty
(1115–1234), 12th to 13th century

National Museums Scotland

Jun ware has long been admired for its mysterious,
glossy opalescent glaze. It fascinated Ming collectors
and connoisseurs and was much admired and written
about in Ming collecting manuals. The simple form
of the elegantly potted bowl above, combined with
the glossiness and sky blue colour of its glaze, which
has pooled on the lower part of the body, typifies
some of the most sought after *Jun* ware qualities
among Ming collectors.

Shen Zhou

Shen Zhou's revival of the literati painting tradition was deeply influential, due in part to his usage of modular composition elements combined with a calligraphic vocabulary of repetitious brushstrokes and dots. This visual vocabulary lent itself to reproduction by literati already trained in the art of calligraphy.

Shen Zhou never took official office, preferring to remain in reclusive filial devotion to his mother at home. Here he engaged in painting, poetry and self-cultivation.

Shen Zhou's painting was influenced by the Five Dynasties (902–979) Nanjing painters Dong Yuan (ca. 934–962) and his pupil Juran (ca. 960–985). This Dong-Ju tradition informed the work of Yuan dynasty (1279–1368) literati painters such as Wu Zhen (1280–1354). Shen Zhou revived this tradition, giving rise to the literati painting tradition known as the Wu school, and in doing so shaped literati painting of the mid-Ming period.

Along with Tang Yin (1470–1524), Wen Zhengming (1470–1559) and Qiu Ying (ca. 1495–1552), Shen Zhou is known as one of the Four Masters of Ming painting.

108
Reading in a mountain dwelling

By Shen Zhou (1427–1509)
Hanging scroll, ink on paper
Height 116.6 cm,
width 28.8 cm
Mid- to late 15th century
Nanjing Museum

109
Idly fishing on an Autumn river

By Shen Zhou (1427–1509)
Hanging scroll, ink on paper
Height 119 cm, width 51 cm
Hongzhi reign (1488–1505), 1491
Nanjing Museum

110
With oars adrift on a lake

By Shen Zhou (1427–1509)
Handscroll, ink on paper
Height 29.5 cm, width 45.7 cm
Hongzhi reign (1488–1505), 1497
Nanjing Museum

秋江閒釣
弘治四年七月洗閱

我愛秋江四壁空
因無別業放孤逢
垂綸大生生涯事
淹唱棹漾野岸風

金北沈公之淺墨秋景其
閒點落生危老氣橫秋
窗況不日校作里南以咏之
丁卯初秋
中溪武生岡

Shen Zhou

The theme of painting 108 – rustic retreat in a remote mountain setting – is one that recurred in Ming literati painting. It was an enduring preoccupation among Ming scholars, who were expected to devote themselves to study for the examination system and government service. The small scale of the scholar in relation to the vastness of the landscape, is typical of Shen Zhou's work.

Paintings such as 109 were not intended to be accurate renderings of an external world, but as metaphors for the inner state of mind and character of the artist. In this painting Shen Zhou evokes the theme so popular in Ming literati painting of boating in a natural setting away from the cares and obligations of everyday life.

The subject of painting 110 – boating in the riverine landscape of the Jiangnan region – became a staple theme of Ming literati painting, evoking a sense of place and an expression of the ideal of retreat from official life amid natural or mountainous settings.

110

Ladies at leisure

During the Ming, painters such as Du Jin (active late 16th to early 17th century) and Qiu Ying (*ca.*1495–1552) revisited the theme of court ladies in a palace setting, but with a greater emphasis on more opulent and detailed architectural backgrounds with which to frame the activities depicted.

The narrative basis can be traced to stories dating to the Han dynasty (206 BC–AD 220), and the way in which a painting such as this was read was likely to be historical. The great gardens of Suzhou, laid out during the Yuan (1279–1368) and Ming dynasties, undoubtedly provided inspiration for the settings observed in paintings of this genre.

111

Ladies in a garden setting

Anonymous hanging scroll, ink and colours on silk
Height 129.1 cm, width 65.6 cm
16th to 17th century
Nanjing Museum

This painting depicts elegant dressed élite or court ladies at leisure in a secluded Springtime garden in which magnolia and cherry trees bloom. In the centre foreground (see opposite), a woman sits reading at a table on which are placed antique bronzes and ceramics of the kind collected and enjoyed by the male literati élite. Other ladies in the painting simply relax and enjoy the beauty of their surroundings.

Many of these paintings, such as the one featured here, without seals or signature inscriptions – the usual attributes of literati art connoisseurship – were produced in Suzhou by professional artists and studios; and it is likely that these genre paintings were created for a primarily female audience.

Ladies at leisure

Court lady paintings, such as this one, are typically set in Spring, as illustrated by the plum and magnolia blossoms, and green willows observed in the painting.

Some activities depicted include those more usually associated with the male literati élite at leisure. These include playing *qin* music, *weiqi* (Go), practising calligraphy and painting, appreciating antiquities and flowers, or convivial drinking. Other activities include *cuju*, a form of football dating back to the Han dynasty (206 BC–AD 220), boating, playing on the swing, and a type of pitch-pot throwing game (*touhu*) where players throw arrows or sticks into a central receptacle.

112

Ladies at leisure in an ancient dynasty

Hand scroll, ink and colours on silk
Height 46.9 cm, width 1361.2 cm
Qing dynasty (1644–1911)
Nanjing Museum

The theme of this handscroll – court ladies in a palace garden setting during Spring – can be traced to painters of the Five Dynasties (902–979), Song (960–1279) and Yuan (1279–1368) periods.

113

Seven-stringed *qin* (zither) inscribed 'the sound of the autumn'

Wood covered with lacquer and inscription
Length 118.5 cm
Ming dynasty (1368–1644)
Nanjing Museum
No image

The *qin* is one of the oldest and most prestigious Chinese musical instruments. Beloved by scholar artists, it was thought capable of conveying the deepest human emotions. Playing it helped to cultivate character and enrich learning. The ideal for Ming scholars was to play the *qin* outdoors in a mountain setting or garden, surrounded by trees and water, and with incense perfuming the air. Two characters inscribed on the back of this instrument translate as 'the sound of the autumn'.

112 [detail of above]

112 [detail of above]

112 [detail of above]

112

112

112

114

Playing the bamboo flute amid pines and streams

By Qiu Ying (*ca.*1495–1552)

Hanging scroll, ink and colours on silk

Height 116 cm, width 65.6 cm

Early to mid-16th century

Nanjing Museum

Qiu Ying

Qiu Ying became the leading exponent of the blue-green tradition of painting during the Ming, which he raised to new levels of sophistication.

Here his painting draws its inspiration from a Tang dynasty (618– 907) poem entitled 'At Chuzhou on the Western Stream' (*Chuzhou Xijian*) by the poet Wei Yingwu (737–792). It describes an unmanned ferry crossing at twilight.

The fine brushwork and use of muted colour in this work is characteristic of Qiu Ying. The blue-green colouration of the landscape consciously refer-ences the archaic 'blue-green' (*qinglu*) style of landscape painting that origi-nated in the Tang dynasty (618–907), and became popular again with the Southern Song (1127–1279) imperial court.

Along with Shen Zhou (1427–1509), Tang Yin (1470–1524) and Wen Zhengming (1470–1559), Qiu Ying is known as one of the Four Masters of Ming painting.

115

Wuyi [Nanjing] *at dusk*

Gu Family embroidery

Embroidered panel, satin with embroidery
and painted colours

Height 66 cm, width 56 cm

16th to 17th century

Nanjing Museum

This embroidery shows the Wuyi Lane, a historic
district in Nanjing. The embroidery is inspired by a
famous poem by the Tang dynasty (618–907) poet Liu
Yuxi (772–842), on the theme of Wuyi Lane at sunset.
Liu's poem describes the noble mansions located here
in earlier dynasties, and the swallows flying above the
eaves of the houses, and Rose-finch Bridge, illustrated
in the embroidery. The embroiderer's use of a poetic
reference is in keeping with the sensibilities of literati
painting.

116

Stone City [Nanjing] *after the snow has stopped*

Gu Family embroidery

Embroidered panel, satin with embroidery
and painted colours

Height 66 cm, width 56 cm

16th to 17th century

Nanjing Museum

The title of this embroidery refers to Stone City. This
was another name for Nanjing, given to it because of
its massive city walls: these can be seen at the right of
the embroidery. A traveller is shown crossing the bridge
on a donkey, with a servant following. The bridge
spans the Qinhuai River which skirts the Nanjing City
Walls. The composition of the embroidery and its
various pictorial elements, recall the literati painting
which had become so influential in the visual arts of
the late Ming.

117

Bathing horses in the shade of willow trees

Gu Family embroidery

Hanging scroll, satin with embroidery and painted colours

Height 124 cm, width 43 cm

16th to 17th century

Nanjing Museum

The subject of this embroidery is the Eight Horses of King Mu (976–922 BC) of Zhou, which relates to an ancient story in which King Mu, wanting to become an immortal, attempts to visit the Queen Mother of the West on a chariot drawn by eight steeds.

Under the preceding Yuan dynasty (1279–1368), leading painters like Zhao Mengfu (1254–1322) and Ren Renfa (1254–1327) revived the use of horse imagery in their paintings, both as metaphors for official service and to flatter the interests of their Mongol overlords.

The subject matter of this embroidery, as well as the format, and the use of a cursive style calligraphic inscription together with seals, all emulate distinctive features of literati painting.

118

Seven Sages of the Bamboo Grove

Gu Family embroidery

Hanging scroll, satin with embroidery and painted colours

Height 125.9 cm, width 55.4 cm

16th to 17th century

Nanjing Museum

The Seven Sages of the Bamboo Grove were a group of scholars, artists, musicians and poets interested in Daoism who lived in the mid- to late 3rd century. They chose to opt out of official life and to reside in the countryside, indulging their interests in drinking and intellectual and artistic pursuits. These individuals provided inspiration for the artists and scholars of later dynasties, seeking to escape the restrictions of official life.

The Seven Sages of the Bamboo Grove became a particularly popular theme in the painting and decorative arts of the Ming.

119

Embroidered panel of an eagle

Embroidery
Hanging scroll, satin with embroidery
Height 121.9 cm, width 57.5 cm
16th to 17th century
Nanjing Museum

This embroidery, in the tradition of Gu Family embroideries, dramatically depicts an eagle perched on a rock below a pine branch and a setting sun.

The image of the eagle was popular with both Ming military officers and officials serving in the Censorate, as the eagle symbolized courage and vigilance. This imagery became highly popular during the late 15th century in paintings by Lin Liang (*ca.*1424–1500), Zhang Lu (*ca.*1464–1538), and others.

In a symbolic and homonymic play on meanings, it acquired specific political intent in the theme known as 'Standing Alone at a Clean Court' (*Qingchao duli*). This is a pun, as the words for 'tide' and 'court' sound identical. An eagle standing alone on a rock amid a surging tide can refer to an isolated official at court standing up for what he believes is right.

Xu Wei

A number of law-suits led to a life of impoverishment for Xu Wei, and he often repaid gifts of food or clothing with paintings.

Xu Wei beat his third wife to death, for which he was sentenced to be executed. He was spared due to the influence of friends.

Freed from prison after seven years, the artist spent much of his last two decades living in a state of itinerant poverty, and he was often drunk. He died at the age of 73.

120
Portrait of Xu Wei (1521–1593)

Portraits of Eminent Men of Zhejiang Province
Anonymous album, ink and colours on paper
Height 45.4 cm, width 26.4 cm
Wanli reign (1573–1620)
Nanjing Museum

Xu Wei was one of the most renowned of Ming painters, dramatists, poets, writers and calligraphers. He painted in a highly individual manner, distinguished by his free use of ink. The expressive and kinaesthetic brushwork noted in the painting opposite is typical of his work.

The painting is signed by the Daoist of Ivy (Qingteng Daoshi), one of Xu Wei's artistic aliases used in later life.

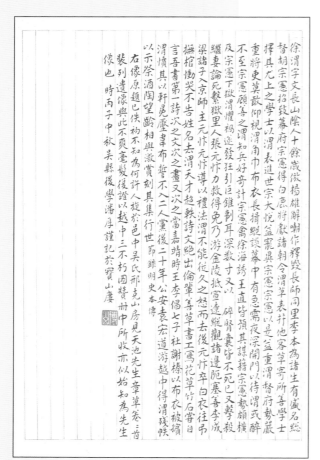

121
Rock, plum blossoms and bamboo

By Xu Wei (1521–1593)

Hanging scroll, ink on paper

Height 104 cm, width 37 cm

Late 16th century

Nanjing Museum

Xu Wei

The subjects of this painting – rock, plum blossoms and bamboo – embody the concepts of perseverance and resilience.

A plum tree and a rugged rock dominate a composition in which contrast plays a key role. The angular branches are captured in broad and frantic strokes, while the blossoms are delicately rendered in fine lines. Plum blossoms were associated with perseverance and purity, blooming on withered old branches after winter. The petals of the flowers represented the Five Blessings – longevity, wealth, health, love of virtue, and a peaceful death.

The painting's poem, in cursive script, outlines Xu Wei's method for painting plum blossoms.

Wen Zhengming

122

Ancient trees and gray mists

By Wen Zhengming (1470–1559)
Hanging scroll, ink and colours on paper
Height 81.5 cm, width 30.5 cm
Jiajing reign (1522–1567), 1530
Nanjing Museum

In this painting, Wen Zhengming emulates the style of the leading Yuan dynasty (1279–1368) painter Ni Zan (1301–1374). Ni Zan's plain and simple landscape paintings were characterized by sketchy brushwork depicting unpeopled landscapes with large expanses of water.

While all these traces of Ni Zan's style are evident in this painting, Wen Zhengming has worked them into a more dense and crowded composition than typically found in Ni Zan's work.

Wen Zhengming

123

Tiger Hill Bridge

By Wen Zhengming (1470–1559)
Handscroll, ink and colours on silk
Height 30.5 cm, width 238 cm
Jiajing reign (1522–1567), 1550
Nanjing Museum

Tiger Hill in Suzhou was a popular site for picnics and outings during the Ming, and remains so today. Even before the Ming, it had long been referenced in the poetry, painting, literature and activities of the literati and cultured élite.

Wen Zhengming has chosen to paint this handscroll in an archaic style referencing the 'blue-green' (*qinglu*) type of landscape painting that originated in the Tang dynasty and became popular once again with the imperial court of the Southern Song.

The depiction of famous sites was an increasingly popular genre in Ming painting, reflecting a growing interest in travel to famous sites. Paintings of such places were not necessarily realistic, but might represent an imaginary tour by the artist.

Wen Zhengming was born in Suzhou. Gifted and versatile, he had a strong impact on mid- and late Ming literati painting.

A pupil of Shen Zhou (1427–1509), founder of the Wu school of painting, Wen Zhengming had many students of his own, including his sons Wen Peng (1497–1573) and Wen Jia (1501–1583).

Wen Zhengming attempted the civil service *juren*-level examinations nine times, but failed. In 1523 he gained a position at the imperial court, but retired in 1527, repelled by the power politics. Thereafter he devoted himself to painting, poetry and calligraphy.

Along with Tang Yin (1470–1524), Qiu Ying (*ca*.1495–1552) and Shen Zhou, Wen Zhengming is known as one of the Four Masters of Ming painting.

Wen Zhengming

This painting is characteristic of Wen Zhengming's late period, where he compressed mountainous landscape compositions into narrow hanging scrolls.

Wen Zhengming's work was highly collectable. The *Treatise on Super-fluous Things – a guide to good taste*, published in the late Ming, includes Wen's work among the first rank of painters: '*These are all famous masters who you cannot be without. It is not appropriate to collect the work of anyone else.*'

Produced at the very end of his life, this work references the painting tradition of Yuan dynasty (1279–1368) literati painting masters Gao Kegong (1248–1310) and Zhao Mengfu (1254–1322).

124

Poetic thoughts in a riverside pavilion

By Wen Zhengming (1470–1559)
Hanging scroll, ink on paper
Height 73.3 cm, width 28.4 cm
Jiajing reign (1522–1567), 1558
Nanjing Museum

125

The demon queller Zhong Kui in a wintry grove

By Wen Jia (1501–1583)
Hanging scroll, ink on paper
Height 54.7 cm, width 23.1 cm
Wanli reign (1573–1620), 1573
Nanjing Museum

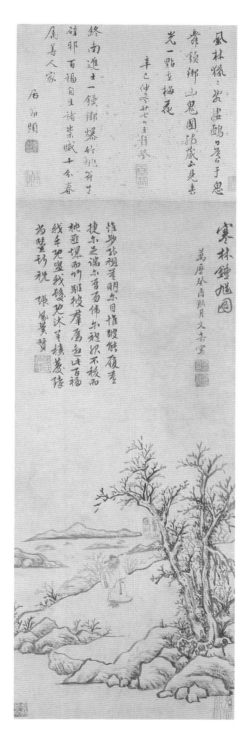

Wen Jia

Wen Jia, the second son of Wen Zhengming, was a gifted painter in his own right. The subject of this work is Zhong Kui, whose grotesque image was used to drive away demons and ghosts. Here he is portrayed more sympathetically as a scholar.

In legend, Zhong Kui achieved top place in the Tang dynasty (618–907) imperial examinations, but because of his ugliness the emperor refused him an official position. In despair, Zhong Kui committed suicide on the palace steps.

Among the various inscriptions on the scroll is one by Zhan Jingfeng, a well-known collector and dealer of the late Ming. It is possible that the painting was sold on the commercial market at some point.

Wen Boren

Wen Boren was greatly influenced by his uncle, the great Ming painter Wen Zhengming.

Rather than attempt the imperial examinations, Wen Boren chose to make his living as an artist, becoming famous for his landscape paintings.

During the mid- to late Ming period, the distinction between the literati or scholar amateur who painted for self-cultivation and the professional artist who painted for money, became blurred.

Lan Ying

Lan Ying (127, opposite) was a painter of the Zhe School. These artists came from different backgrounds to the élite amateurs of the Wu School.

Most had been employed at some time by the imperial court as professional painters. However, the unrestrained and elegant strokes of Lan Ying's late work owe much to the work of Shen Zhou.

126
Path amid pines and jutting boulders

By Wen Boren (1502–1575)
Hanging scroll, ink and colours on paper
Height 85.5 cm, width 36 cm
Mid-16th century
Nanjing Museum

127
Playing chess opposite Spring Mountains

By Xie Shichen (*ca*.1487–*ca*.1567)

Hanging scroll, ink on paper

Height 120 cm, width 62.2 cm

Early to mid-16th century

Nanjing Museum (no image)

Xie Shichen came from a well-to-do family in Suzhou. His work has been mistaken for that of Shen Zhou, the great master of the Wu school. It is possible that he was a student of Shen.

Xie Shichen was a versatile painter and calligrapher and well known for his large-scale landscapes. This scroll depicts the typical idyll of the scholar artist – lofty mountains, knotty trees and secluded dwellings.

128
Orchids and rocks

By Lan Ying (*ca*.1585–1664)

Folding fan, ink on paper

Height 18.9 cm, width 55.3 cm

Chongzhen reign (1628–1644), 1632

Nanjing Museum

Lan Ying was a professional painter rather than an élite amateur. This fan depicts a type frequently painted as well as collected by Ming literati for their studios and gardens.

Folding fans offered a small-scale but public means of displaying painting and calligraphy. Although intended as a fan, many literati fan paintings were bound into albums. The scale of the work also made it suitable for modest gifts or commissions. The fan, however, was not widely used as a format until the 16th century.

Currency

Copper coins and silver ingots remained the preferred forms of currency throughout most of the Ming. An ingot featured in the exhibition is worth 50 ounces or *liang* and would have been the heaviest in circulation. A Ming *liang* was equivalent to 37.5 grams.

129

Paper banknote representing one silver ounce

Woodblock printed ink on paper
Height 33 cm, width 21.5 cm
Hongwu reign (1368–1398)
Nanjing Museum

Paper money was issued during the Ming between 1373 and 1522, after which it was discontinued. The denomination of this banknote is one *guan*, nominally equivalent to 1000 copper coins. All Ming banknotes, regardless of when printed, bore the reign name of Ming founder, Hongwu.

At the very end of the Ming, in 1643, the government faced a shortage of funds and began printing banknotes again. They were referred to as *feiqian*, literally 'flying money'.

129

130

Zun-shaped flower vase with archaic decoration

By Hu Wenming (late 16th century)
Cast and partially gilded bronze and silver inlay
Wanli reign (1573–1620)
National Museums Scotland

This bronze flower vase bears an inscription with the name of Hu Wenming, a renowned late-Ming craftsman who produced bronze vessels. Based in the Jiangnan region, Hu's vessels consciously catered to literati antiquarian tastes by imitating the forms and designs of ancient bronze artefacts. His work was greatly sought after amongst those who aspired to and emulated a literati lifestyle.

131

Bianhu moon flask with decoration of magnolias

Jingdezhen, Jiangxi province
Porcelain with underglaze blue
Yongle reign (1402–1424)
to Xuande reign (1426–1435)
National Museums Scotland

This form of flask is known as a *bianhu* (in English, 'moon flask') and was probably used to store wine. It features a decoration of magnolia blossoms on the body, and a ring of downward-pointing banana leaves around the base of the neck. Equivalent forms were also found in glass and ceramic in the Middle East. The appearance of this form – along with a number of others produced by early Ming potters – is likely to have been inspired by vessel types found in Islamic culture.

132

Cloisonné incense-burner with animal-shaped handles

Gilded copper alloy and polychrome enamel inlays and lotus flower decoration

Width 14.4 cm, height 9.4 cm

Jingtai mark and reign (1450–1456)

Nanjing Museum

This cloisonné incense-burner features a continuous pattern of scrolling lotus flowers in five different colours against a blue ground. The form of this incense-burner is derived from an ancient bronze ritual vessel known as a *gui*. Cloisonné altar and ritual offering vessels used during the Ming followed both imperial and textual conventions that required such vessels to be based on ancient bronze examples. The archaic form was often combined with decorative styles contemporary to this period.

133

Cloisonné vase with floral decoration

Gilded copper alloy and polychrome enamel inlays

Height 14 cm, diameter (foot) 5 cm

17th century

Nanjing Museum

This cloisonné bottle features a continuous pattern of scrolling red, blue and yellow lotus flowers against a blue ground. Lotus flowers remained a consistently popular motif on Ming cloisonné of all periods, either individually or combined with other decorative and auspicious motifs. The lotus flower is a traditional motif of Buddhist iconography. The inspiration for its use is likely to have come from the floral and foliate scrolls used by porcelain painters on 14th-century blue and white ceramics.

134

Cloisonné incense-burner with dragon-shaped handles

Gilded copper alloy and polychrome enamel inlays

Diameter 9.6 cm, height 8.3 cm

Jingtai mark and reign (1450–1456)

Nanjing Museum

The central roundel on the body of this incense-burner contains the character *shou* in red, expressing a wish for longevity. It was part of a large repertoire of decorative motifs used by Ming craftsmen across many media. It was a particularly popular decorative pattern on items intended as birthday gifts.

135

Cloisonné plate with decoration of birds and flowers

Cast copper alloy with polychrome enamel inlays and decoration of birds and flowers

Diameter 27.5 cm

Mid-Ming dynasty (1368–1644), 15th to 16th century

Nanjing Museum

The central roundel of this cloisonné plate features the design of a bird on a branch surrounded by magnolia and plum blossoms. Plum blossoms and magnolia are both associated with the end of Winter and arrival of Spring. Bird-and-flower designs such as this one had their origins in painting and began to appear in Ming cloisonné from the end of the 15th century.

136

Fish vat with decoration of dragons

Jingdezhen, Jiangxi province
Porcelain with underglaze blue decoration of dragons chasing a pearl
Jiajing mark and reign (1522–1567)
National Museums Scotland

This large vat was used for raising fish and aquatic plants in the imperial palace or palace gardens. It is painted on the outside with two imperial dragons chasing a flaming pearl. The dragons and floral motifs have been outlined and then painted between the lines with iron-rich cobalt which produces a very dark blue. This iron-rich imperial quality cobalt was imported at great expense from Persia and Central Asia.

137

Dish with foliate rim and floral decoration

Jingdezhen, Jiangxi province
Porcelain with underglaze blue floral decoration
Diameter 34 cm
Yongle reign (1402–1424)
National Museums Scotland

The decoration of this dish is typical of early 15th-century porcelain from Jingdezhen, with its prominent floral style.

The central roundel contains a design which includes lotus, peony, chrysanthemum and camellia blossoms within a floral scroll. Further floral designs fill the broad border below the rim. The foliate rim of this dish has a scrolling pattern of crested waves.

THE MING ECONOMY
AND THE ENCOUNTER WITH THE WEST

明
代
王
朝

The Ming attitude to foreign trade

Ming trade, diplomatic, political and cultural relations with surrounding peoples and states were formally administered under the tribute system. The Ming received tribute and in turn granted gifts, imperial favour and recognition of sovereignty primarily in the Sinitic world, but also extending to states and peoples in Southeast Asia.

During the early Ming period, the emperors of the new dynasty adopted an expansionist stance in their dealings with states and peoples beyond their borders. The early 15th-century sea-voyages of the eunuch Admiral Zheng He (1371–1433) to Southeast Asia, South Asia, the Middle East and East Africa, which took place under the Yongle emperor (r.1402–1424) were aimed at extending the influence and hegemony of the new dynasty.

Seven voyages were undertaken between 1405 and 1433, each of them enormous in scale. The first in 1405 consisted of a fleet of 317 ships, with crews totalling almost 28,000. It is traditionally believed that these were the largest wooden ships ever built, and estimates for the size of the largest nine-masted 'treasure ships' of the fleet are put at 127 metres in length – five times the size of the 24-metre *Santa Maria* sailed in by Christopher Columbus (1451–1506) in his voyage of discovery to the Americas several decades later.

Zheng He's ships brought many goods from China to trade and gift, including large quantities of tea, textiles, lacquer ware, silk and porcelain; and in return brought back many tribute goods and gifts from the various places visited during the voyages. Most famously, in 1414 a giraffe from the King of Malindi (in modern-day Kenya) was presented to the imperial court from the King of Malindi (in modern day Kenya). It was believed to be a *qilin*, a mythical unicorn, which was interpreted as a validation of the Yongle emperor as Son of Heaven.

During the three decades of Zheng He's voyages, Ming China greatly extended its sphere of influence into the Indian Ocean, gaining geographic knowledge and returning with foreign goods, but the voyages never resulted in any conquered territory or Ming colonial footholds. And with the death of the Yongle emperor in 1424, Zheng He's voyages were vehemently opposed by Confucian officials at court, most notably the senior official Xia Yuanji (1366–1430), as an unnecessarily costly vanity project. Only one further voyage was permitted after the emperor's death, and all future voyages cancelled after the demise of Zheng He: even the records of the voyages were destroyed in 1477.

With the ending of these voyages, and increasingly preoccupied by the Mongol threat on its northern border, Ming China turned away from external engagement. Due to its great wealth, power and resources, the imperial court felt little need to trade with other nations. Maritime trade was thus heavily restricted and foreign trade officially allowed only through tribute missions. However, private trade continued, and despite the Ming court reaffirming its ban on maritime trade over 30 times during the 15th and 16th centuries, and several times attempting to destroy any ships made for foreign travel, foreign trade continued.

Large trading networks developed in coastal southeast China and trade with Southeast Asia, Japan and Korea flourished. Smuggling was rife and many literati serving as government officials in coastal regions turned a blind eye to the realities of maritime trade, realizing that trade lessened piracy. However, the pressure to trade with other nations only intensified, and in the late 16th century the imperial court finally acknowledged this, and the reality of European traders appearing on its shores, by partially lifting the ban on trade in 1567. Trade from Fujian was now allowed, although trade with Japan was still banned. A system of licensed private traders was set up, and penalties for those engaged in unlicensed maritime trade were severe, including beheading. Piracy, which had always been a problem along the Chinese coast, had by the mid-16th century become endemic and large scale.

Late Ming encounters with maritime Europe

Early 16th-century European maritime expansionism led to direct shipping routes opening between Europe and East Asia, and Portuguese traders became the first Europeans to establish direct contact with the Ming during the 16th century, first arriving on China's south coast in 1517. But it was only in the 1570s that the Portuguese finally managed successfully to establish a foothold on Chinese territory at Macao. Despite resistance from the imperial court, the Portuguese were followed by the Spanish, and then the Dutch in the early 17th century, each bringing New World silver to trade for Chinese goods.

Demand for Chinese goods, from Europe, Southeast Asia, and Japan was boundless, and Japanese silver did much to stimulate and prepare the 16th Ming economy for the vast influx of New World silver that followed the discovery by the Spanish of vast silver reserves in Peru in the 1540s. The Portuguese, Spanish and then Dutch sought tea and especially silk, textiles and porcelain. By the early 17th century as much as half of all silver leaving the Spanish silver mines in Peru and Mexico was entering the Ming economy in exchange for Chinese goods.

The discovery of the New World by Christopher Columbus in 1492 would come to affect profoundly the Ming economy, population, agriculture and eventually the Ming relationship with the wider world. From the mid-16th century, New World crops which reached China via the Philippines – including potatoes, tomatoes, chillies, peanuts, maize and sweet potatoes – began, along with improved rice strains, to radically transform Chinese cuisine and agriculture, leading to a healthier population and facilitating the rapid growth of the population in the late 16th and 17th centuries.

Proselytizing European missionaries soon followed the opening of trading routes between Europe and China, almost all from Catholic orders. The most successful of these, in terms of their interaction with and understanding of Chinese culture, were the highly educated and learned men of the Society of Jesus, the Jesuits, who made considerable efforts to master the Chinese language, to understand Chinese culture, and to accommodate the understanding of their faith within a Chinese cultural framework by using existing Chinese concepts. Among the qualities which made the Jesuits comparatively more success-

ful than the other Catholic orders in China, was their cultivation of Chinese literati and ruling élite, use of European art, books, and visual resources, and a training in Greek and Roman classical culture which equipped them with an outlook open to dealing with non-Christian cultures. The Jesuits did succeed in making some converts to Catholicism, although they faced considerable obstacles in doing so. All Chinese religious and belief traditions were polytheistic and Christian notions of a single God were among a number of Christian concepts that proved difficult to translate into Chinese terms.

They also brought with them the latest European knowledge of astronomy, artillery, cartography, mathematics, clock-making, medicine and a range of other subjects. As a result, they greatly interested and intrigued the Ming intellectuals they encountered and were regarded as foreign literati (although they also encountered suspicion and hostility among Ming officialdom).

The most extraordinary of these remarkable men was the Italian Matteo Ricci (1552–1610) who arrived in China in 1583 along with another Italian Jesuit, Michele Ruggieri (1543–1607). Ricci had developed a system of remembering extensive quantities of information by assigning each item of information to a different room within an imagined house. This allowed him to not only to learn to write Chinese in an age before bilingual dictionaries, but also to memorize the Four Books (*Sishu*) of the Confucian Canon, an astonishing feat since these titles total around 50,000 characters.

Eventually, Ricci and Ruggieri obtained permission to open a house in Beijing, and Ricci was appointed as an advisor on scientific matters to the imperial court in 1601, for which he received a stipend, becoming the first European to visit the Forbidden City to which he was given free access. Ricci set a precedent for later Jesuits to serve in the Directorate of Astronomy (*Qintian jian*), and in a variety of other roles at court including painters and book translators.

The beginnings of the porcelain export trade

Jingdezhen in northern Jiangxi province had been a site of ceramic production for both the Chinese and export markets since the Song dynasty (960–1279). Although located inland, it was ideally situated near high quality sources of raw material, forests for fuel, and waterway networks for transport and shipping. During the early and mid-Ming, Jingdezhen's imperial factory kilns produced huge quantities of the highest quality porcelains for the imperial court. By the late 16th century, orders from the imperial court were in decline, but an expanding cash economy and booming population during the same period resulted in Jingdezhen becoming increasingly commercial and market-orientated in its output. A growing number of privately-run businesses and kilns in Jingdezhen began catering to both the domestic and export markets, and after 1608 when the Wanli emperor (r.1573–1620) decreed that the imperial kilns were to be closed, private kilns dominated output at Jingdezhen.

The arrival of Portuguese and then Dutch traders offered new markets over the course of the 16th and early 17th centuries, and the first large quantities of Ming porcelain began to reach Europe in the early 17th century. With so much experience supplying the imperial court, domestic market and various Asian and Middle Eastern export markets, Jingdezhen's innovative potters quickly adapted to supply European decorative tastes and vessel forms.

The production of porcelain, especially blue and white, led to the greatest and most obvious interaction and exchange between Chinese and European visual forms and mediums, and the aesthetic of Ming blue and white porcelain would exert great influence on European and world ceramic traditions. Demand quickly grew for the exotic luxuries of Chinese tea, silk and skilfully painted porcelains with intense shades of blue against a white background. The first porcelain type to reach Europe in great numbers was the thinly-potted *Kraak* ware with its heavy

figurative and naturalistic blue and white decoration usually applied in a spontaneous, freely-brushed style. The rims were prone to chipping and it was considered too light and inferior for the domestic market, but was suitable as an export ware. It was produced primarily at Jingdezhen, as well as at a few other smaller kiln sites in southeast China.

Kraak was mass-produced in vast numbers from the late 16th century until the 1640 and it quickly came to define Chinese porcelain in the market-places of Europe. The term *Kraak* is thought to have come from the Dutch term for the Portuguese merchant ships of the period known as *caracca* – referred to as a 'carrack' in English – although it only appears to have been commonly applied after 1675. The association with Portuguese *caracca* appears to lie with the capture by the Dutch East India Company of two such Portuguese vessels in the South Atlantic – the *Sao Tiago* and *Santa Caterina* – in 1602 and 1604, the contents of which were then auctioned off in Amsterdam.

Within two decades, porcelain was reaching Europe in such quantities that it had become affordable by the middle classes, and by the 1630s wooden models of European vessels – such as tankards, mustard pots, butter dishes and salt cellars – were being sent to Jingdezhen to allow the potters there to copy them.

Porcelain was considered a truly remarkable material in 17th-century Europe with the secret of its production only finally discovered in Meissen in 1708. Porcelain is made from porcelain stone (*baidunzi*) and kaolin (gaoling or China clay), and fired at temperatures higher than 1300°C to produce a white vitreous ceramic which is impervious to liquids and stains, especially when glazed, and which provides an decent surface for underglaze or over-glaze decorations. The result is a material which is attractive and easy to clean as a tableware, and also fulfilled a decorative function in European interiors, as seen, for example, in the Dutch still-life paintings and paintings of interior from the early and mid-17th century.

As Europe produced little that Ming China needed, silver was used for payment. This led to enormous quantities of New World silver entering the late Ming economy, and completely transforming it into a monetized economy. The trade in Chinese porcelain grew exponentially, and the records of the Dutch East India Company (V.O.C. or Vereenigde Oost-Indische Compagnie) established in 1602, show that 16,000,000 pieces of porcelain were exported from China to Europe by its ships between 1602 and 1682.

Jingdezhen continued to export to other markets such as Russia, Japan and Southeast Asia, and these exports were at least as substantial as those of the European trade, underlining the industrial scale of production at Jingdezhen. Despite the vast quantities of porcelain exported from late Ming China, it only ever represented a tiny percentage, estimated at less than two per cent, of the value of the Asia trade in which other goods such as spices, silk, and textiles were far more valuable. However, it is surviving pieces of porcelain which offer the most tangible evidence of the late Ming encounter with European market demand.

FURTHER READING

Brook 1999; Brook 2005; Brook 2010; Butler and Wang 2006; Chang and Chang 1992; Finlay 2010; Kang 2010; Levathes 1996; Mann 2011; Mungello 2014; Rinaldi 1989; Spence 1985; Ströber 2013; Wills 2011

138

Jar with decoration of pines, bamboo and plum blossoms

Jingdezhen, Jiangxi province

Porcelain with underglaze blue of pines, bamboo, and plum blossoms

Height 22.3 cm

Wanli mark and reign (1573–1620)

Nanjing Museum

This jar is decorated with the Three Friends of Winter consisting of pine, plum blossom and bamboo, with the pine repeated twice (see page 17). Each plant has been painted with its stems or branches contorted into variations of the character *shou*, meaning longevity.

139

Meiping (plum vase) with decoration of peacocks and peonies

Jingdezhen, Jiangxi province

Porcelain with underglaze blue decoration of peacocks and peonies

Height 40.5 cm

Zhengtong reign (1436–1449)

Nanjing Museum

Although from Jingdezhen, this vase was not produced in an imperial factory kiln, but in an ordinary production kiln.

The main band of decoration around the vase depicts peacocks among peony flowers. Peacocks and peonies have been associated with royalty and nobility in Chinese literature and art since at least the Tang dynasty (618–907). The secondary bands on the shoulder and around the foot show patterns of scrolling floral motifs and banana leaves.

140

Hexagonal vase with floral decoration

Jingdezhen, Jiangxi province

Porcelain with underglaze blue floral decoration

Height 37.3 cm

Wanli mark and reign (1573–1620)

Nanjing Museum

This double-eared hexagonal vase is a product of the imperial factory kilns at Jingdezhen. The open-work ears on the neck are an unusual and rare feature. The neck and body of the vase are decorated with dense floral patterns, with two registers of flowers within panels on the body, including peonies and other blossoms. A Wanli-era reign mark is visible just under the rim of the vessel.

141

Dish with floral decoration

Jingdezhen, Jiangxi province

Porcelain with underglaze blue floral decoration

Diameter 54.7 cm, 10.3 cm

Jiajing mark and reign (1522–1566)

Nanjing Museum

The exterior of this large dish features an underglaze design of pine, plum blossom and bamboo. These three plants endure through winter and are known as the Three Friends of Winter (see page 17).

A flower scroll design with quatrefoil blossoms occupies the dish's central roundel. The surrounding band is decorated with four sprays of chrysanthemum, peach, peony and pomegranate. In between is a falling leaf from each spray, and a flying insect. A six-character Jiajing reign mark can be found just under the rim.

142
Lianzi (lotus-seed) bowl

Jingdezhen, Jiangxi province
Porcelain with underglaze blue
decoration
Xuande mark and reign (1426–35)
National Museums Scotland

Porcelain from the reign of the Xuande emperor
had become highly collectable by the late 16th
century. Those who aspired to the literati
lifestyle paid high prices for certain types of
porcelain from this era.

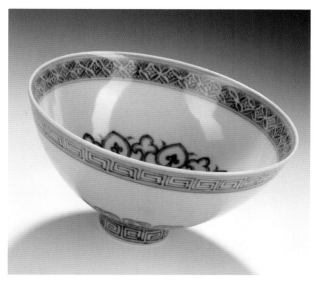

143
Kraak ware 'crow cup'

Jingdezhen, Jiangxi province
Porcelain with underglaze blue
decoration
Early 17th century
National Museums Scotland

This *Kraak* ware bowl is popularly known as
a 'crow cup' (*kraaikoppen* in Dutch). A bird
resembling a crow can be seen on a rock in the
centre medallion, hence the term 'crow cup'.
In fact the bird, with its head arched back to
look at the moon, is a magpie (*Xique*), which
is considered a lucky bird in China.

Kraak porcelain

Kraak is the Dutch word for a type of blue and white ware produced mainly for export at privately-owned kilns in Jingdezhen between 1550 and 1650.

When a decline in imperial orders forced the Jingdezhen kilns to source other markets, it was produced in vast quantities for markets in the Middle East, Southeast Asia, Japan, and finally Europe.

Kraak probably comes from the word given to Portuguese carraca ships (*carracks*) of this era, the first vessels to bring such ware to Europe. It was generally considered too poor quality for the domestic Chinese market.

Characteristic features include radiating panels with naturalistic motifs, busy decoration, plentiful use of cobalt and thin bodies with rims prone to chipping.

144

145

146

144

Kraak ware plate with underglaze blue decoration

Jingdezhen, Jiangxi province

Porcelain with underglaze blue decoration of deer and floral motifs

Diameter 21.5 cm, height 4 cm

Wanli reign (1573–1620)

Nanjing Museum

145

Kraak ware plate with underglaze blue decoration

Jingdezhen, Jiangxi province

Porcelain with underglaze blue decoration of floral motifs

Diameter 28.8 cm, height 5.3 cm

Wanli reign (1573–1620)

Nanjing Museum

Plates 141 and 142 are typical of the *Kraak* ware which began to arrive in Europe in the early 17th century.

146

Bowl with underglaze blue decoration of *lingzhi* mushrooms

Jingdezhen, Jiangxi province

Porcelain with underglaze blue decoration of *lingzhi* mushrooms

Diameter 14.5 cm, height 7.3 cm

Wanli mark and reign (1573–1620)

Nanjing Museum

This bowl is decorated with a type of mushroom known in Chinese as *lingzhi*, associated with longevity and immortality in Daoist iconography.

Wanli shipwreck

The objects on the previous page were all salvaged in 2005 from the 'Wanli Shipwreck', found off the coast of Malaysia.

The ship was European, probably Portuguese. It went down in *ca.*1625 with a cargo of 37,000 Ming ceramics on board, after being sunk by a Dutch ship.

Ceramics recovered from datable wrecks provide valuable information about the forms, types and the decoration of Ming ceramics.

147

Map of the myriad countries of the world

By Matteo Ricci (1552–1610)
and Li Zhizao (1565–1630)

Ink and colours on paper

Height 168 cm, width 382 cm

Wanli reign (1573–1620), 1608

Nanjing Museum

This 1608 map reproduces a version produced in 1602. The 1602 map was originally drawn by the Italian Jesuit Matteo Ricci (1552–1610) in collaboration with the Chinese mathematician and cartographer Li Zhizao (1565–1630).

Although there are distortions and inaccuracies in the map, it conveys a great deal of knowledge about what was then known of the world based on 15th and 16th century European trade and exploration. The map includes brief annotations, in Chinese, of regions and countries, their fauna and peoples. It also includes astronomical information on solar and lunar eclipses.

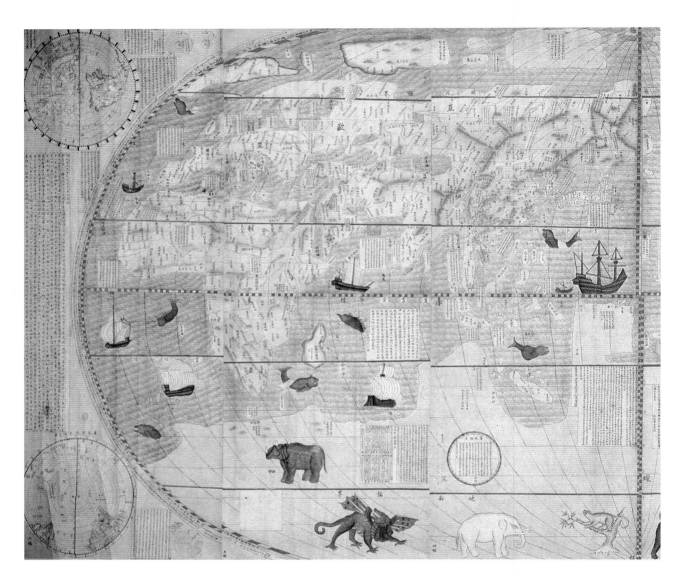